Black Appetite. White Food.
Issues of Race, Voice, and Justice Within and Beyond the Classroom

Black Appetite. White Food. invites educators to explore the nuanced manifestations of white privilege as it exists within and beyond the classroom. Renowned speaker and author Jamila Lyiscott provides ideas and tools that teachers, school leaders, and professors can use for awareness, inspiration, and action around racial injustice and inequity.

Part I of the book helps you ask the hard questions, such as whether your pedagogy is more aligned with colonialism than you realize and whether you are really giving students of color a voice. Part II offers a variety of helpful strategies for analysis and reflection. Each chapter includes personal stories, frank discussions of the barriers you may face, and practical ideas that will guide you as you work to confront racial injustice in your classroom, campus, and beyond.

Jamila Lyiscott is a social justice education scholar, nationally acclaimed speaker, spoken word artist, and educational consultant. She serves as an assistant professor of Social Justice Education at the University of Massachusetts Amherst, where she is the co-founder and director of the Center of Racial Justice and Youth Engaged Research. She also holds an appointment as Senior Research Fellow within Teachers College, Columbia University's Institute for Urban and Minority Education.

Black Appetite. White Food.

Issues of Race, Voice, and Justice Within and Beyond the Classroom

Jamila Lyiscott

Routledge
Taylor & Francis Group

NEW YORK AND LONDON

First published 2019
by Routledge
52 Vanderbilt Avenue, New York, NY 10017

and by Routledge
2 Park Square, Milton Park, Abingdon, Oxon, OX14 4RN

*Routledge is an imprint of the Taylor & Francis Group,
an informa business*

Library of Congress Cataloging-in-Publication Data
A catalog record for this book has been requested

ISBN: 978-1-138-48065-0 (hbk)
ISBN: 978-1-138-48066-7 (pbk)
ISBN: 978-1-351-06238-1 (ebk)

Typeset in Palatino
by Apex CoVantage, LLC

Contents

Acknowledgments

For Jehovah Nissi; Brian and Charmaine Lyiscott; Jeanette Lyiscott; Valentine Ferdinand; Lucille Ferdinand; Celestine Lyiscott; Nicole Dyer; David E. Wilson and the Kings Church of Christ; Moriah McDuffie; Angela Collins; Maya McDuffie, Miles McDuffie my aunts, uncles, and cousins in Trinidad and Cali; Dyahnah Wilson; Christina Cater; Sharifa John; Shakira John; Michael Cirelli, Urban Word NYC; Cyphers for Justice; CNV; David E. Kirkland; Ernest Morrell; Yolanda Sealey-Ruiz; Marc Lamont Hill; Christopher Emdin; Ryan Parker; and Justis Lopez. For Trinidad and Tobago; for Crown Heights and Bed Stuy Brooklyn, New York; for the African Diaspora. For the countless names of those in the village that raised me.

Meet the Author

Jamila Lyiscott is a Harry Potter enthusiast, a community engaged scholar, a nationally renowned speaker, and a spoken word artist. She is currently Assistant Professor of Social Justice Education at the University of Massachusetts Amherst, where she serves as the co-founder and director of the Center of Racial Justice and Youth Engaged Research. Jamila also holds an appointment as Senior Research Fellow of Teachers College, Columbia University's Institute for Urban and Minority Education. Across these spaces, Jamila's work focuses on racial justice, community engagement, and youth activism in education through the lens of what she has termed "Vision-Driven Justice." She has been invited to more than 100 institutions throughout the nation where she works with youth, educators, and people across disciplines to inspire vision and action. Her scholarship and activism work together to prepare educators to sustain diversity in the classroom, empower youth, and explore, assert, and defend the value of Black life. As a testament to her commitment to educational justice for students of color, Jamila is also the founder and co-director of the Cyphers For Justice youth, research, and advocacy program, apprenticing New York City high school youth, incarcerated youth, and preservice educators as critical social researchers through hip-hop, spoken word, and digital literacy.

Jamila is most well known for being featured on Ted.com, where her video, *3 Ways to Speak English*, was viewed over 4 million times, and for her commissioned TED Talk, "2053" in response to the inauguration of the 45th president of the United States. She has also been featured in Spike Lee's "2 Fists Up," on NPR, the *Huffington Post*, Lexus Verses and Flow, Upworthy, The Root, and many other media outlets nationally and internationally. Her poetry and scholarly work have been published in several peer-reviewed scholarly journals.

*"...because God hath caused me
to be fruitful in the land of my affliction."*

—Genesis 41:52

A Note to the Reader

Black Appetite. White Food. is rooted in the tension of excellence and erasure. Of access and assimilation. Of classrooms that too often demand that Black and Brown students shed their magic at the threshold of schooling in order to be palatable to whiteness. Our appetite deepens for the rich cultural diversity that should be at the center of every students' educational experience across the nation. Yet, the course of schooling remains the same.

I will speak of race, and hope, and pain, and rage, and tangible possibility. I will use poetry, experience, narrative, and scholarship. This will not happen neatly. It will not fit into a box. Sometimes I will say "yo," or "son" (because I am from Brooklyn). Sometimes I will say "hegemony" (because I am from Predominantly White Institutions). I will break form and I will conform, and each decision is intentional.

In the spirit of Roxanne Gay, who proclaims herself to be a "Bad Feminist," full of blind spots and contradictions in her commitment to Feminism, I begin here with the proclamation that I am a bad scholar, a bad activist, and a bad educator. Rather than what may be viewed as self-deprecation, I find freedom in this. That is, in my commitment to equity, hope, and justice, especially in the contexts of race and education, I consider every iteration of my work to be unfinished and partial, awaiting the supplementary questions, experiences, and push-back that are beyond my capacity as one being in the tapestry of humanity.

I, therefore, speak from what I do and what I know as a poet, critical social researcher, educator, and Black woman millennial at the same time as I relish in the infinite incompleteness of my own knowledge. Does this mean that the pages to come lack rigor, depth, and utility? Frankly, no. For the past 15 years

I have dedicated my life to deep social inquiry and advocacy around questions of racial justice and education. My work has taken place first in the form of community-based organizing and teaching, in-school and out-of-school social justice professional development workshops for New York City–based educators and then in the form of directing national social justice education conferences, major research projects leading to publications, the completion of my doctoral degree, university-based teaching, and viral media appearances. Finally, these experiences have worked together so that over the past two years I have been invited to more than 100 schools, universities, conferences, and community-based organizations across the country to work directly with P–20 educators, students, faculty, and administrators to address issues of race and education.

In my work with these hundreds of educators across the country, I have found too many stuck in anxiety, fear, guilt, or apathy or with the thought that racism is not their problem to solve. Much like my childhood moments of deepest opposition— when my parents gave me way too many chores to do at once, which, instead, inspired me to do nothing—these educators find the task of "fixing" racial issues wildly overwhelming. Some articulate to me that the journey of uprooting white privilege1 feels too abstract and monumental to be tangible. Others communicate that they are eager and willing and just want to know where to start. I have yet to visit a space where the topic of racism and privilege did not evoke palpable emotion or blatant discomfort, pointing to the overwhelming social significance of the topic within and beyond the space of school.

The purpose of *Black Appetite. White Food.* is not to convince you that white privilege exists, that it exists malignantly, or that it pervades our systems of education on both macro and micro levels. If you are reading this book, then my assumption is that you already believe at least some of these things and are now ready to take action in the service of dismantling white privilege. The purpose of this book, rather, is to serve as a tool for *concurrent* analysis, action, and advocacy against white privilege as it functions within your respective spheres of influence: concurrent because there is a false binary between analysis and action, between activists and theorists, as though one can act responsibly without the deep method of thought or as though one can analyze social phenomena relevantly without active engagement in our social realities; concurrent because too many who wish for racial justice are shackled by stagnant analysis with the thought that they must fully know and understand everything about whiteness, privilege, and race before they can ever take action against it. My approach to this work is process-oriented rather than outcome-oriented. So, in order to do this work, you will not need to know everything about whiteness and white privilege before taking action. In order to do this work, you will need to abandon any notion of neat categorizations, of fixed meanings, and of sweeping victories with shiny bows on top.

In order to do this work, you have to be willing to sit in the inevitability of discomfort that accompanies authentic confrontation, to accept that disrupting something as abiding and pervasive as white privilege will have its costs, and to rest on the conviction that "the arc of the moral universe is long, but it bends toward justice."

Finally, in order to do this work you will need to visualize what you are fighting *for*. When it comes to the work of social justice, we often become so consumed by what we are fighting against that we hardly take the time to truly envision the kinds of schools, communities, and societies that we are fighting for. I have been personally guilty of this. As I actively engaged in a range of protests across the country throughout 2014–2015 in the Black Lives Matter movement, I found myself in poorer and poorer health. In my commitment to taking action *against* anti-Blackness to ensure that Black lives matter, I neglected to matter to myself. My energy was trapped in a cyclical response to racial hatred, and it became important for me to determine what I was fighting *for* as I fought *against* white privilege and intersecting systems of oppression that work together to sustain inequity. If I was fighting for Black lives to matter, then space and time had to be reserved to visualize and embrace what the fullness of that would mean for me and our world. In fact, responding to white privilege at the expense of actualizing a tangible vision for a world outside of white privilege was, indeed, re-centering and reifying white privilege. What is alarming is the fact that since the United States has never known a history without white privilege, most of us can hardly muster up a vision for a future that does not depend on this toxic ideology. Yet visualization— the act of constructing a palpable vision of what you aspire to become—is a central practice for the world's highest performers across disciplines. Perhaps you have witnessed and/or perpetu- ated some of the deepest ills of white privilege in your classroom, school, and community. Will you be driven by the passion to confront racism, bigotry, systemic violences, and hate? Or will you be driven by a tangible vision for your classroom, school, and community as white privilege is confronted across these spaces? I say we need both.

I invite you to be infinitely unfinished and partial in this work alongside me as we step into the enmeshed messiness of analysis, action, and advocacy *for* a better world.

Note

1. My decision to not provide a fixed definition of white privilege in the book is an intentional invitation for you to illuminate and grapple with the understandings that you bring to the table. Since we are always making meaning, and meaning is always shifting, I invite you to explore the myriad existing definitions of white privilege to inform your evolving understanding of the concept.

Introduction

Dear Teacher,

Before you teach us to splinter our souls
For a seat at the table
Teach us to splinter our hands
As carpenters of our own justice

How dare you engorge us
With this feast of feeble freedoms
While our appetites remain
An unquenched black whole

"I refuse to be the face of color on the brochure of this school while I experience unaddressed racism here every single day!" The 16-year-old young lady in front of me is ready to burst into tears. I had been flown out to her predominantly white private school in an elite community on the Pacific coast of California to address more than 600 6th- to 12th-grade students on issues of race and racism on campus. The group of students who fought for funding to bring me out, and who were made up exclusively of student leaders of color on campus invited me to an intimate lunch session to wrestle with the questions they did not feel safe asking in the larger assembly. "Why should I participate in their false representation of racial equality here?" she continued. "My mother says it's the least I could do since they've given me a scholarship to be here, but I don't owe them anything! And because I am known for taking a stand on campus, I've become the target of open racist comments yet the school does absolutely nothing about that." As the young lady bursts into tears and is consoled by another member of the student group, I feel emotions well up in my throat. I am here for one day. What could I possibly say or do to support this group of teenagers who should have the freedom to agonize over their college applications but are occupied instead with the racial climate of their school and by questions of who will possibly continue their efforts toward racial equity once they graduate? As we stare out together across the perfectly manicured lawns of the campus and the questions hang in the air for more time than feels natural, I look at each of the students and the one staff member who works to sustain the campus group, and I say, "Thank you so much for who you are and for everything you continue to do."

How will your classroom be remembered on the other side of the history that we are inscribing at this very moment? Fifteen years into the future will your students recall a space where the rampant racial injustices of our society went unacknowledged in your classroom? Where the different racial identities in the room and the dynamics associated with these differences went unaddressed? Where the content of the curriculum ignored the cultures of their communities? The previously mentioned student will recall the trauma of a racist high school experience. This will singe into the sinews of her journey from adolescence into adulthood as she fights to understand her "self" in relation to her world. She will recall little to no refuge in her classrooms and a school where few educators and administrators had the courage to acknowledge that one of our nation's deepest festering wounds, white privilege, inevitably impacts the everyday lives of students of color, especially in predominantly white contexts.

The time for inscribing new futures is now. The authority to author new, more equitable social realities belongs to each of us. In our high-stakes testing society, our focus on quantitative outcomes, such as test scores, reading levels, and the like, exemplifies our failure to see how deeply racial anxieties suffocate the souls of students, robbing them of healthy learning environments. Our obsessive focus on outcomes is an inherent flaw in our traditional approach to the litmus test of student wellness and educational success. And these measures of success, having their roots in Eurocentric standards, values, and traditions, are imposed on students of color as a barometer of their deservingness for full humanity. As a critical social researcher, I have come to understand the everyday realities within the space of school is saturated with under-acknowledged racial tensions. These tensions are at times brimming in the public imagination following viral videos of racial violence or a sociopolitical landscape littered headlines which reflect the unabashed racism of our country's leaders. The sub-heading of a 2015 *Washington Post* article titled "Racism in Schools is Pushing More Black Families to Homeschool their Children" reads, "Eurocentric school curricula continue to prevail in a society that is increasingly brown."[1] Our failure to illuminate the dangers of the white privilege coursing through America's veins and the arteries of our schools position white privilege as neutral, normal, standard, and benign as it pushes students and their families to the margins of true educational access. Along with the overt violences that emerge within a society that positions whiteness as rightness, white privilege has so long shrouded us in the lie of its glory that we fail to see one of its most obvious limitations: that without exposure to the powerful cultural, linguistic, and historical differences that exist within diverse cultures, our students will be severely limited and underprepared global citizens in our richly diverse world.

My experiences working alongside dozens of communities, schools, and universities across the nation to confront the manifestations of racism and white privilege at their institutions have had some striking similarities. The issues playing out across these institutions reveal a deep hunger for change throughout the United States:

1. The racial elephant in the room! More than 85% of urban educators are white in the face of an increasingly multiracial, multicultural, multilingual student body.

Although the racial differences between teachers and students affect the social space of classrooms, the everyday dynamics associated with these differences are rarely, if ever addressed.

2. Lack of diversity in curriculum and pedagogical approaches. One 16-year-old Native American student who has joined the social action efforts emerging out of Standing Rock shared that when she questioned her history teacher about why there was only one paragraph covering Native American history in the whole textbook, she was sent to the principal's office.

3. Ignorance about how to deal with overt (much less covert) racial tensions as they manifest themselves in the classrooms and broader institutional contexts. During one of my "3 Ways to Face White Privilege" workshops, a teacher nervously articulated her ignorance: "If I see white privilege manifesting itself in my classroom, as an educator I don't know how to address it and students may see my lack of action as accepting the mistreatment that occurs." In another instance, a group of undergraduate students who invited me to build with them for a few days on their Predominantly White Institution campus in North Carolina shared that a series of hateful chalkings targeting the university's small immigrant population emerged across the campus. Although reported several times, nothing was done to address it.

4. Can this and should this work be done interracially or within affinity groups? Efforts to address institutional racism often center the needs and concerns of white participants, with the expectation that people of color will openly showcase their painful narratives in order to educate everyone else.

These and many other concerns have remained consistent across the institutional spaces I have worked with. In many cases, collectives of students/educators have already begun to organize and take action in light of these issues. In these instances I also found patterns in the challenges that emerged in the face of action. Some of these patterns include the following:

1. The few People of Color (students, teachers, administrators, etc.) committed to combatting racial injustice in the institution were simply burned out. White privilege is heavy and exhausting alongside the work of trying to just be fully human with an everyday load of work and life. This is referred to as Racial Battle Fatigue.

2. Anyone even wishing to engage in racial justice work conceived of it as an uphill battle of extra and more exhausting work given the pressures from administration to uphold standardized curriculum and teach toward tests.

3. The white people who were willing to engage in the work were presumptuously taking up too much space in these efforts. In order for the work to be done, willing white participants wished to remain comfortable or to prove that they are not racist, or they are overridden with guilt and emotions about the issues of racism. All of these work to center white privilege.

4. White participants were immobilized by the fear that any of their attempts to address racism would be viewed as racist. And in this fear emerged white silence alongside the expectation for people of color to carry out the emotional labor connected to this work: to tell our stories, to prove, to teach, to cry out, and to reveal the ugly underbelly of our pain for other people's learning.

5. The larger institutional context, with a thin veil of political correctness around allowing such efforts to thrive felt starkly different from the energy of these groups. These siloed initiatives (often mandatory diversity trainings or Black history month efforts) were allowed to exist but often struggled to penetrate the larger school

communities in ways that felt the most necessary—to confront the people in power to ally themselves against institutional-level white privilege.

This is not to say that these were helplessly desperate groups awaiting my arrival to save their schools from racism. It was clear in each and every encounter that I was a student of their rich experiences, incremental successes, abiding questions, and personal testimonies at the same time as I came to help deepen the sustainability of their work as much as possible. The patterns were so profound that I decided to start documenting my experiences. Written reflections and detailed notes about repeated questions, anxieties, and indicators of successfully undoing racism all came to inform this book.

Today, the true work of addressing white privilege at the classroom level are minimal and lack sustainability. Even within school spaces full of educators, administrators, and superintendents of color, the policies, curricula, and general ethos of in-school spaces are deeply rooted in Eurocentric white middle class frameworks, values, and standards.

This book rests on the conviction that we all have the capacity to be complicit in perpetuating white privilege. If we are not careful to attend to the ways that the insidiousness of whiteness functions systemically and beyond its connection to white skin we will be eternally off target in our efforts to confront it.

Optional Activity

Facing Tough Questions
  ◆ Listen to "Will You Be My Black Friend," (https://bit.ly/2QC0Rdh) episodes #1701-a and #1701-b of *Our National Conversation About Conversations About Race.*
    ◆ Who is responsible for addressing the issue of white privilege as it plays out in your classroom? School? Community?

- ◆ Who do you feel safe discussing racial injustice with?
- ◆ Within your institutional space will the work of addressing white privilege need to happen within affinity groups or interracial contexts or not? Why?

Note

1. Mazama, A. (2015, April 10). Racism in schools is pushing more Black families to homeschool their children. *Washington Post*. Retrieved from: https://www.washingtonpost.com/posteverything/wp/2015/04/10/racism-in-schools-is-pushing-more-black-families-to-homeschool-their-children/?noredirect=on&utm_term=.862f6ecbc2ff

Part I
Naming the Problem

1

Vision-Driven Justice

Healing is not the absence of pain
It is the decision to act
In the service of your development
Rather than your defeat

I am a Harry Potter enthusiast. This might be one of the most important things to know about me. During Harry's first year at Hogwarts School for Witchcraft and Wizardry, he stumbled upon a mysterious mirror. The mirror, hidden away, and only discovered by Harry because of his knack for always gettin' into some mess, was called "the Mirror of Erised." When Harry first stood in front of the mirror he was startled to see that alongside his reflection, his late parents, Lilly and James Potter, stood smiling and waving. Harry rushed to wake up his best friend, Ron, so that he, too, could see Harry's parents in this magical mirror. But when Ron came to the mirror, he did not see Harry's parents at all. Instead, he saw, along with his own reflection, an older version of himself decked out with accomplishments that he could only dream of. I am a Harry Potter enthusiast because author J.K. Rowling must herself be a magical being to so poignantly and piercingly forge such powerful moments of deep personal reflection in the world of her stories. You see, Harry found himself in front of that mirror every single night, staring into the eyes of his parents who passed away when he was just 1 year old. He sat there lost in the mystery of this mirror until the sagacious Dumbledore found him one night. At this point in the story, we learn from Dumbledore that what the Mirror of Erised does is show ones "deepest and most desperate desires." By standing in front of this mirror, one is confronted with their heart's deepest wants, which for Harry, was to have his mother and father in his life. But then Dumbledore offers a crucial warning when he says to Harry, "this mirror offers neither knowledge or truth . . . men have wasted away in front of it . . . that is why I am having it removed."[1]

If my 15-year-old self were to stand before the Mirror of Erised, weighing 259 pounds at 5 feet tall, with dark brown skin and glasses, I would have seen a slim, shapely teenaged young woman, with long, flowing hair and hazel eyes. Transfixed, I would have been immobilized by this cruel apparition of my imagination. I would watch it. It would watch me. A prison of desire. I would have been powerless to walk away and mold the life I wanted, too stuck to step away from the mirror and into my journey. In my life, I have spent plenty of time trapped in the hauntings that Rowling speaks of through the story of this mirror. Being confronted with the realities of my deepest desires, interrogating those desires, and then powerfully stepping into the complexity of my journey knowing that I am forever unfinished has been the stuff of me. In reality, the deep impact of my childhood obesity would wrap itself up and through my Blackness and my womanhood like a sprawling ivy. My perception of the world would find its grooves most saliently along the contours of my body type, my racial identity, and my gender. Most Black parents of young girls in America are forced to have the "you're Black-and-woman-and-you-have-two-strikes-against-you" talk.

In my mother's eyes, I could see another fear, one that fell in harmony with the historical figurations of mammies that mark Black American history. I was a dark chocolate Black girl suffering from obesity, and this reality is central to my story. Here, within the intersecting margins of my world, I had to dig deep to define myself outside of the social mirror. My lens as a scholar-activist today was forged in the trenches of some of my hardest childhood moments. My ability to critically question how institutions (de)value certain bodies and cultures was made in raw moments of needing to forge my own sense of worth and beauty outside of social standards. My fierce compassion for equity was brewed in real moments of defiance, of defining my fullest humanity in the face of a world that works to attach deep shame to dark Black women without the right body type.

This is my story. I share it because if you are an educator who has never faced their story as it intersects with the various social locations that shape how you show up in our schools and in our world, then you are destined to do this work irresponsibly. What are the stories that shaped your view of the world? What people and places socialized you into accepting the norms and values that script your life either knowingly or unknowingly.

If you were to stand before the Mirror of Erised, what would you see?

What hopes...

What pain...

What deep and desperate desires...

The question is a paradigm shift for many of us who are used to approaching social justice work in ways that are strangely divorced from personal wellness work. Stephen Covey (2004)[2] refers to paradigms as maps of how we view the world. Our current paradigms for social justice work broadly rarely prioritize the immediate shifting realities of our mental health, family dysfunction, triggers, traumas, and all of the heavy things that impact how we show up to our classrooms. But before we can enter into a conversation about what it means to broach the sociopolitical struggles of racism and white privilege, we must enter into a conversation about how *you* navigate struggle within your self. Our personal histories matter deeply to our capacity to contribute to social justice so that what Yolanda Sealey Ruiz refers to as 'the archaeology of the self,' is a crucial excavation process for us all.

When I was 10 years old, my father taught me how to ride a bike on Empire Boulevard in pre-gentrified Crown Heights, Brooklyn. Well . . . he attempted to. I sat on my bright pink bike, and over and over again gravity defeated me as I fell sideways onto the ground. Eventually, in a Trini accent as thick as cassava, my father said, "Jamila, yuh have balance?" How would I know? I looked at him confused, and understanding my expression he directed me to "stand on one leg." After a few attempts, I finally found some semblance of balance on one leg. "Get back on de bike," he said after a few minutes of my awkward attempt to find stability on one foot. When I got back onto the bike, to my shock, I rode straight down the block. What my father taught me in that moment is that if I did not have balance within myself, how in God's name could I expect to have balance outside of myself?

Many of us leave homes where the most toxic, unbalanced relationships fester as they intersect with our personal mental health issues, childhood trauma, triggers, and systemic oppression and then enter into our classrooms confused about why we cannot find balance in any aspect of our work. How in the world are you going to address the sociopolitical systemic magnitude of racial injustice without deep self-awareness of how to navigate your own personal struggles? *Social* justice requires personal wellness. Public impact requires private introspection.

Take a few minutes to enter into this visualization exercise with me. This exercise, inspired by Adele's "Hello," came to me after reading an interview where Adele shared that the song "Hello" is more than a romantic love song. She shared that this song was essentially a message to herself saying, "Hello from the other side of what I have been through." After reading this interview, I developed the following visualization exercise, which I have been blessed to lead people through all over the country. Each time the room is full of tears, and deep emotion, and we are then ready to embark on true dialogue and action toward racial justice.

Take a moment in a quiet space by yourself, to think of a struggle that you are navigating in your life right now. It may be a struggle that is invisible to the rest of us, but it is palpable for you. It may be a struggle that you feel is insurmountable . . . it has loomed over your life for years . . . its teeth have a grip on your past and are gnashing at your future.

After you can think of this struggle very clearly, close your eyes, and visualize yourself on the other side of that struggle. Who is the "you" that has overcome this seemingly endless mountain? What do you look like on the other side? How do you feel in your body? Who is that person? Make it real.

Now after you've conjured up this version of yourself in your mind, take a few moments to write a letter to yourself of today from yourself on the other side of your struggle. Do this before you read any further.

Most people find themselves in a state of pain, hope, rage, possibility, confusion, and catharsis after doing this exercise. How can all these polarized emotions exist at the same time? It is because, once you speak to the version of yourself on the other side of what you are going through, that person is likely compassionate, championing you and giving you a roadmap of what it takes to get over! It is that roadmap that is the key!

What will our world look like on the other side of white privilege?

This exact question was on my heart in the days, weeks, and months following the 2016 election. So when I opened my e-mail on an early January 2017 morning, I was pleased to see a message from the folks over at TED inviting me to write and record a poem at their headquarters. The election results for the 45th president of the United States produced a muggy social climate.

It felt sticky. Cloudy. Uncertain. Who could have forecasted this? The people who reached out to me from TED certainly did not. The tone of the email was "we need . . . something . . . some word . . . some words . . . some hope . . . something to offer the nation in this deeply divisive moment." No pressure!

I gladly accepted the invitation. The resulting TED Talk, "2053," imagines how we will look back on this historical moment in the year 2053. In the face of such deep national struggle, I needed to find hope . . . from our selves on the other side of this history. The final line of "2053" is

> healing is not the absence of pain. It is the decision to act in the service of your development, rather than your defeat.

Vision-driven justice is a paradigm shift that requires you to enter into a deep, honest assessment of who you are, where you are, and what you are up against as you fight toward who you need to become. This process of self-awareness means that before you can enter into social justice work . . . Before you trip yourself up with an ego-driven approach to justice that is rooted in a white savior complex or an internalized inferiority complex that low-key reiterates white supremacy, you have to be honest about your private and personal stuff, your "stuff" as it intersects with your social identities (i.e., race, class, gender, language, etc.), and your social identities as they map themselves onto your motivations, habits, and behaviors that may lead you to the point of having the best intentions for changing the course of racial justice but the worst approach.

Healing is Not the Absence of Fear

The trick about gearing up to change yourself and to change the world is that . . . it's too much! The pain you'll have to endure, the uncertainty of the outcomes, the fear of loss, the lack of tools that you are sure about, the chaos of working with people across lines of political and social difference . . . dis tew much! You're right. It is too much. Change is a lot. Think about what it felt like to speak to that person on the other side of your struggle . . . even after such a powerful conversation, taking the first step forward can feel impossible. The fear of changing yourself is not far off from the fears that come up as you truly think about changing your classrooms and, even more, changing the course of white privilege as it manifests itself in your part of the world. On top of all this, a true fight for racial justice requires those who benefit and find comfort in white privilege to give something up. These are big questions, but throughout my time working with educators, many fears about endeavoring to see and confront white privilege within themselves, relationships, and institutions have come to light. Some common concerns are the following:

◆ What if I become a target in my school and risk getting fired?

◆ What if my attempts to confront white privilege are viewed as racist?

◆ What if my family stops speaking to me because I finally say what's on my mind when they are being racist?

◆ What if I reject white privilege and embrace my racial identity as a person of color and then I lose opportunities/access?

◆ What if a parent comes up to the school and doesn't like what I have been teaching my students after I change my curriculum?

◆ What if I offend my friends of color by asking them uncomfortable questions about race?

◆ If white people shouldn't ask people of color about racism, who are we supposed to talk to?

◆ What if I call out white privilege in my PWI as the only person of color and I am dismissed as crazy, angry, or problematic?

I could fill several pages with the questions and fears that emerge among educators who want to know how to confront white privilege but are afraid to move forward. To address both the validity and absurdity of these fears, I draw from Brendon Burchard's *The Charge*. Brendon Burchard's *The Charge* is a *New York Times* bestselling book that focuses on personal development goals for its readers to reach their maximum potential in life. During my own personal reading of this text I came across a powerful chapter about the fear of change. Although ...I made sure to make my own personal applications, because the work of addressing social injustice in education is always on my heart, I could not help but make connections to the questions, anxieties, and testimonies of the educators I had been working with for years. I draw on Burchard's "fear of change" conceptions to encourage your reflection on anything that might hold you back from the fullest engagement with your journey toward confronting white privilege. I have found, that articulating fears on the front end, makes addressing the obstacles in the way of our vision much easier. According to Burchard[3], there are three types of fear that stop people from engaging in (social) change:

1. Fear of *loss pain*: Here, Burchard argues that in the face of (social) change, we tend to focus more on what we might lose than what we might gain, and so we do not move forward.

2. Fear of *process pain*: Here, Burchard argues that in the face of (social) change, we tend to focus on the inevitable pain of any worthy process as something that will defeat us rather than develop us.

3. Fear of *outcome pain*: Here, Burchard argues that in the face of (social) change, we tend to visualize negative outcomes instead of visualizing positive outcomes.

Vision-driven justice means that self-awareness is combined with the deep ongoing social awareness of what we are up against (including our fears) and a tangible palpable vision of what we are authoring into our collective futures.

My personal definition of oppression is being trapped in someone else's narrative with no power of authorship. This definition thrives in the ways that the narrative of white supremacy has authored Blackness as dirty and delinquent, Indigenous as uncivil and cannibalistic, Latinx as parasitic, and the list goes on and on. This definition serves as a lens into understanding the ways that Black and Brown bodies remain trapped in other people's narratives of what educational success, achievement, and brilliance must look like. A narrative authored by white privilege and reinscribed by the norms and standards that we have yet to disrupt. Perhaps, this definition can be better understood through the fable of the man and the lion who were having an argument in the jungle about who is strongest. The man argued, "I am stronger than you, I'm the king of the world!" and the lion argues, "I am stronger than you, I'm the king of the jungle!" until they stumbled on a picture. The picture featured a man killing a lion. The man pointed at the image and exclaimed, "You see! I told you, I am stronger than you," to which the lion replied, "Yes, I see. But who drew that picture?"

Notes

1. Rowling, J. K. (1998). *Harry Potter and the Sorcerer's Stone*. New York: Arthur A. Levine Books.
2. Covey, S. R. (2004). *The 7 Habits of Highly Effective People: Restoring the Character Ethic*. New York: Free Press.
3. Burchard, B. (2012). *The Charge: Activating the 10 Human Drives That Make You Feel Alive*. Florence: Free Press.

2

Black Appetite. White Food.

"But how can white people not know that they have white privilege? I mean, come on!" The end of a workshop about race and racism in the classroom with a group of 11 New York City high school teachers is thick with tension. The teachers in the room have already self-identified their racial categories (white, Black, Latinx, and Asian) and have been in the throes of using some of the new tools I have shared to willingly grapple with the impact of white privilege on their classrooms for the duration of the workshop series. The not-so-rhetorical question was thrown out by a Black woman who could not understand the possibility of white people being genuinely ignorant about the toxicity of whiteness. Nervously, a white woman, face flushed, chimed in: "Well, sometimes it's unintentional. Like, I have friends of color so I'm aware of the things that are problematic to say or do, but one time I brought a friend of color to my mom's house, and my mom made such a racist comment. She had no idea, she is a loving, good woman, but I know my friend and I knew immediately that he was uncomfortable." I sat back and let the conversation take its natural course. In my approach to facilitation in such spaces, it is more important to *create space* for people to wrestle with difficult racial questions that we rarely have the opportunity to discuss openly than for me to pretend that I have come with some fixed singular answer to the question of white privilege. Eventually, I did enter the conversation: "What a privilege it must be to not know that white privilege is a problem after hundreds and hundreds of years of people of color protesting racism with their bodies, voices, pens, ballots, across digital landscapes, and more. If centuries of cries against white privilege have truly fallen on deaf white ears, then we are in far more trouble than I ever imagined." My words are direct and inevitably create discomfort in the room. But by now we have intentionally created space for discomfort as a necessary precursor of authentic dialogue. We have cultivated a space that is sacred and brave with the knowledge that this work cannot happen unless we are willing to abide in the tensions we are afraid of. We are clear that discomfort means something different for people with racial privilege and people without it. We do not shy away from these truths. Most importantly, by now I have already made it clear to all the participants that my goal is not to reify white privilege by coddling the comfort levels of the white folks in the room. For now, we will sit in the crosshairs. *Black Appetite. White Food.*

Black appetite? White food? In such a diverse society where we seek to regard the complexity and humanity of all racial groups, why does everything always have to be so black-and-white?! And why are we talking about appetite and food in a conversation about racial justice and white privilege?! We exist in a society where white privilege is sustained and engages people of color (the "Other") inasmuch as people of color function to spice up the dish of whiteness. Following Beyoncé's loss to Adele at the 2017 Grammys for song, record, and album of the year, Beyoncé's younger sister Solange Knowles tweeted, "There have only been two black winners in the last 20 years for album of

the year. There have been over 200 black artists who have per-
formed."[1] Ongoing issues of cultural appropriation, including
Indigenous and blackface Halloween costumes also reveal our
society's consumer relationship to non-white racial groups as
whiteness continues to be our main course.

The metaphor of appetite and food goes beyond white-
dominant culture's parasitic consumption of other racial groups.
Imagine that we have made it to the point where every racial
group across the world has made it to the world's table. The table
is round. There is no head. There is no hierarchy. Just every racial
group at the table on equal standing. However, the table is *always*
overladen with a European feast. In a world that has suffered
the ills of imperialism, colonization, and slavery . . . imagine
that we have all finally fought our way toward "access" to the
table, yet the substance of what is served is still steeped in the
privileges of whiteness. How can we say that our students have
"access" in a society that saturates media, politics, institutional
practices, curriculum, pedagogy, and policies with white middle
class values as the sole course of substance? As our appetites
long for a world that affirms plural racial and cultural identities
as equally valuable, we are force-fed whiteness in our everyday
lives at the expense of the rich capacity for our differences to
powerfully shape our world. In my time working with a group of
teachers on confronting their own internalized white privilege,
several teachers realized, for the first time, that they could not
recall reading one book written by a person of color throughout their entire educational journeys. These were graduate students. In 2009, Texas State Representative Betty Brown publicly
announced that Asian Americans should adopt names that are
"easier for Americans to deal with."[2] Months later, I watched a
17-year-old Asian American poet address a spoken word piece
to Betty in tears. With the knowledge that by "American," Betty
truly meant "white," he shared that his name had been changed
to an "American" one at so young an age that he could not
pronounce his original Korean name properly. He mourned that

he couldn't speak to his own grandmother anymore since she spoke no English. As he indicted Betty's blatant racism, what unfolded in the piece was a deep appetite for a culture he and his siblings had lost as their parents worked to erase their names and language for a safer and more successful transition into "American" culture. In *every* workshop or class where I have shared the words of this poem with people of color, one or more of the participants hold a testimony that aligns with the story of this young man.

The Black-White Binary

Within America's collective consciousness—as complex and developed and progressive and critical as we imagine ourselves to be—is a deeply engraved binary: the purity of whiteness against the putridness of Blackness. Home to an abundance of racial and ethnic groups, at its core, in the United States racial formation and subsequent racial categories continue to measure racial groups across a spectrum where both inter- and intraracial politics occur in relation to whiteness as desirable and Blackness as problematic. Across communities of color in America, for example, internal stratifications of beauty position lighter skin, softer/straighter hair, and leaner bodies as the most desirable (i.e., closer to white aesthetic standards), whereas darker skin, coarser hair, and curvier body types (i.e., closer to generalized depictions of Blackness) are viewed as less beautiful. In India Arie's *Songversation* she shares,

It's all based on Eurocentric beauty ideals: For example; Straight, blonde hair, blue eyes, aquiline nose, thin limbs, lighter skin . . . for many this is just considered "beauty." Why? Because eurocentric aesthetics are seen as the standard, and therefore are more palatable and desirable by the world as a whole. The entertainment industries are no exception, they SELL this desire to the world. MOST publications lighten darker people, because lighter skin and hair reflect more light and are more eye catching, magazines are after all a business.[3]

This is not just an American construct. A history of European colonization and imperialism has imbued a global consciousness that bends toward the aesthetics and values of whiteness so that the value of one's social standing is measured by one's proximity to it. Of racial formation in the United States Omi and Winant write,

> In the United States, the black/white color line has historically been rigidly defined and enforced. White is seen as a "pure" category. Any racial intermixture makes one "nonwhite." In the movie *Raintree County*, Elizabeth Taylor describes the worst of fates to befall whites as "havin a little Negra blood in ya' just one little teeny drop and a persons all Negra."[4]

We must look this fundamental racial binary in the face in order to illuminate the massive social construct that we silently exist within—a racially stratified Black–white continuum. That racial identity is a social construct does not make it any less real or harmful to our world. Indeed, the act of reading that you are engaged in, in this very moment is a socially constructed activity. To openly acknowledge that the socially constructed sanctity of whiteness was forged against the stigma of Blackness in America is to take the first step toward grappling with the historically rooted binary that this book seeks to disrupt. Omi and Winant move us to a deeper historical understanding of how this binary came to be:

> In the United States, the racial category of "black" evolved with the consolidation of racial slavery. By the end of the seventeenth century, Africans whose specific

identity was Ibo, Yoruba, Fulani, etc., were rendered "black" by an ideology of exploitation based on racial logic—the establishment and maintenance of a "color line. . . . With slavery . . . a racially based understanding of society was set in motion which resulted in the shaping of a specific *racial* identity not only for the slaves but for the European settlers as well." Winthrop Jordan has observed: "From the initially common term *Christian*, at mid-century there was a marked shift toward the terms *English* and *free*." After about 1680, taking the colonies as a whole, a new term of self-identification appeared—*white*.[5]

The formation of "black" and "white" categories during U.S. chattel slavery had a lasting significance on American society and continued to evolve across the national landscape throughout the 18th, 19th, and 20th centuries. After slavery, the Black–white binary was crucial to social order upheld by legislation. By the mid-19th century, America was home to an onslaught of poor European immigrants who faced profound discrimination and criminalization alongside continued legal discrimination against Blacks. Fixated on the Black–white binary, however, social scientists endeavored to assimilate these immigrant populations into whiteness. At the University of Chicago, social scientist Charles R. Henderson declared in one of his first textbooks, "the evil of [immigrant crime] is not so great as statistics carelessly interpreted might prove," but where the "Negro factor" is concerned "racial inheritance, physical and mental inferiority, barbarian and slave ancestry and culture," were among the "most serious factors in crime statistics."[6] By the middle of the 20th century, European immigrants were assimilated into the category of "white" while people of various phenotypes and genealogies were relegated to the category of "black" determined by the one-drop rule. As European immigrants were humanized and ushered into the privileges of whiteness, Blackness "became a more stable racial category in opposition to whiteness through racial criminalization."[7]

Throughout American history, racial categorization has occurred along the spectrum of this Black–white continuum. Black criminalization is the currency of white privilege. Globally, racial politics play out differently from region to region so that someone categorized as "black" in America might be categorized as "colored" in South Africa, a marker with its own sociopolitics rooted in the history and context of South Africa. In some countries, racial categories have less importance than other social locations, such as class and religion. What is alarming, however, is that despite these nuances, anti-Blackness is global, and all over the world whiteness is a powerful signifier of privilege and hierarchy. To dismantle white privilege, we must wrestle with this ideological fixture. We must uproot the languages, practices, and habits of knowing and being that play on the presence of this fixture in our minds, and we must attend to how the intraracial politics among people of color play into and resist this fixture in myriad ways.

Entering the Discourse

Developing the skills to define, identify, and address the various manifestations of white privilege as it plays out in our world is crucial. For example, in the vignette, catering to what is referred to as "white fragility" would have resulted in a situation that upheld white privilege even as it tried to combat it. In an article that discusses "white fragility," DiAngelo (2011) writes,

> White people in North America live in a social environment that protects and insulates them from race-based stress. This insulated environment of racial protection builds white expectations for racial comfort while at the same time lowering the ability to tolerate racial stress,

leading to what I refer to as White Fragility. White Fragility is a state in which even a minimum amount of racial stress becomes intolerable, triggering a range of defensive moves. These moves include the outward display of emotions such as anger, fear, and guilt, and behaviors such as argumentation, silence, and leaving the stress-inducing situation. These behaviors, in turn, function to reinstate white racial equilibrium.

(DiAngelo, 2011, p. 54)[8]

Another feature of white privilege that emerges in the preceding vignette is an insistence on viewing *intention* as more *important* than impact. By sharing that her mom is a "good" and "loving" woman, the workshop participant sought to assure us that her mom's *intentions* were in no way malicious. In an episode of MTV's *Decoded* titled "5 Things Everyone Should Know About Racism," Franchesca Ramsey shares the problem with white people's focus on their intentions as more important than the impact of their racist actions. Ramsey asks us to imagine that someone has accidentally stepped on your foot. While the *intent* was not malicious, the *impact* of the injury still hurts and so needs to be addressed by the person who inflicted it. This simple example seeks to illuminate the ways that many white people seek to evade their complicity in upholding and benefitting from white privilege. Among the most common frustrations that I have encountered is that white privilege is so normalized that it is hard to see for some, that when it *is* seen they are terrified to point it out for fear of being ostracized, and that when they find the rare space to point it out, they have no idea what to do about it.

In "Peculiar Benefits," Roxane Gay, defines privilege as

a right or immunity granted as a peculiar benefit, advantage, or favor. There is racial privilege, gender (and identity) privilege, heterosexual privilege, economic privilege, able-bodied privilege, educational privilege, religious privilege and the list goes on and on. At some point, you have to surrender to the kinds of privilege you hold because everyone has something someone else doesn't.[9]

Throughout the chapters, I offer some examples of how white privilege manifests itself in our world, but the purpose of this book is not to define white privilege. The purpose is to create space for you to define and enter into deep conversation with meanings and manifestations of white privilege, especially as it manifests itself in your school, community, and yourself. As a central part of engaging in the frameworks for analysis, action, and advocacy that I offer, I encourage you to continuously immerse yourself in the texts, testimonies, historical resources, community organizations, and so on at your disposal that theorize the features of white privilege. It's also important to know, that as a Black woman, I speak, research, write, and act from the powerful experiences tethered to my racial and cultural identities. That's a fancy way of saying that my work is very unapologetically Black. I used to believe that in order to be committed to racial justice, I had to have deep knowledge of all racial groups. The truth is that because race is a social construction, Blackness is not monolithic, and I cannot even speak on behalf of all Black people, even if I tried. So I come to you with theories and examples that have emerged organically out of my experiential knowledge, my passion for exploring the African Diaspora, and with the hope that each and every one of you might be inspired to do the similar work in ways that feel authentic to you.

Optional Activity

In order to address white privilege within and beyond schools, it's important to start with a working definition of *white privilege*. Because language constantly falls short of approximating meaning, wrestling with terms as they have been theorized, on one hand, and as we understand them in our everyday realities, on the other hand, is crucial. Within any given space with say, 12 teachers, there may exist 12 different understandings of white privilege. While some might find this over-whelming, I find it useful. The moment that we can acknowledge our roles in constructing, reinforcing, and misunderstanding the definitions of social locations such as racial identity, we understand our complicity in social reproduction and our capacity to engage in social disruption.

Materials Needed:

◆ Index cards or sticky notes
◆ Pen or pencil

Professional Development Activity:

◆ Distribute three to four index cards/sticky notes to each person in the room.
◆ Step 1: Working individually, write one word that comes to mind when you think of "white privilege" on each index card/sticky note. (5 minutes)
◆ Step 2: In small groups of three share out each word and your thought process as you chose them. (5 minutes)
◆ Step 3: As a small group of three, group or map out all your words in a way that makes sense to the group. (7 minutes)
◆ Step 4: Using just one index card/sticky note, attempt a one- or two-sentence definition of *white privilege* that emerges from your conversation and the words you've chosen. You may use words that you haven't listed to create your definition. (7 minutes)
◆ Step 5: Share in a large-group discussion.

Importantly, these definitions should be considered *alongside* text-book and other definitions of terms. The goal is to start here but to become committed to building knowledge and self-awareness about white privilege throughout our lives. I emphasize the fact that I position textbook definitions "alongside" working definitions to impress our roles as an *agents* of social change. What do I mean by this? If you enter the conversation of white privilege with a textbook definition to govern the work, several things will happen: (1) You will not have the opportunity to unearth and confront your understanding of white privilege and its limitations; (2) we will reinforce the idea that the only valid producers of knowledge are scholars or other elite members of society who have rarely, if ever, stepped foot into a classroom like yours; and (3) you will fail to view yourself as someone who can and must produce, disrupt, and confront definitions and their impact for a better world.

Notes

1. https:/ thefader.com/2017/02/13/solange-grammys-response-beyonce-lemonade
2. https://chron.com/news/houston-texas/article/Texas-lawmaker-suggests-Asians-adopt-easier-names-1550512.php
3. https://colorismhealing.org/colorism-quotes/
4. Omi, M., & Winant, H. (1994). *Racial Formation in the United States: From the 1960s to the 1990s*. New York: Routledge.
5. See endnote 4.
6. Muhammad, K. G. (2010). *The Condemnation of Blackness: Race, Crime, and the Making of Modern Urban America.*
7. See endnote 6.
8. DiAngelo, R. (2011). White Fragility. *International Journal of Critical Pedagogy*, 3(3).
9. Gay, R. Peculiar Benefits. See https://therumpus.net/2012/05/peculiar-benefits/

3

If You Think You're Giving Students of Color a Voice, Get Over Yourself!¹

Miss, miss! What the C.O. toldju about us? They already gettin' in y'all heads right? Miss, we human! I'm a human! We have families. . . .
—Rikers Island Youth Workshop Participant

The walls on Rikers Island are the same as the walls in my high school. In a facility six security check-points deep, where it takes myself and my team of social justice educators over 1.5 hours to get from the first screening to the classroom where we run a workshop with a small group of incarcerated adolescent boys, the walls are the same style of brick as every inner-city school I have ever attended or visited. While I am struck by the visceral effects of this very concrete reality for these young men who have attended public schools across the five boroughs, I am not at all surprised. Still, within the physical, psychological, and emotional confines of this space that they navigate daily, I am the one who often feels the deep constraints of internalized social attitudes and perspectives about young Black and Brown men, who they are, what they need, and how they should be engaged within the context of the classroom. The possibilities of our time together are tethered to my internal work—the shedding of any savior complexes and constant collective reflection with the team to live in the tensions and questions of our work as critical educators.

So imagine my horror when on a recent phone call, a white educator who expressed interest in my youth development work squealed with congratulations and awe for the way that we "give so many young people voice." Her words were deeply disturbing but hardly surprising. Grateful that in our last e-mail I chose the "phone call" over the "in-person" or "FaceTime" option for our meeting, I rolled my eyes and promptly ended the call.

I should not have ended this call. I should have said to this woman was "If you think you're giving students of color a voice, get over yourself," then hung up the phone.

So what's the big deal? Why get caught up on words when you know that kind, well-meaning woman only meant to celebrate the work that you are doing?

Some of the most deeply problematic issues of inequity within the field of education are sustained by well-meaning people embracing progressive politics without intentional frameworks of self-reflection to guide their praxis in a healthy direction.

Here's the Problem

1. **It's paternalistic.** Webster's defines *paternalism* as "the attitude or actions of a person, organization, etc., that protects people and gives them what they need but does not give them any responsibility or freedom of choice?" The idea of "giving" students voice, especially when it refers to students of color, only serves to reify the dynamic of paternalism that renders Black and Brown students voiceless until some salvific external force gifts them with the privilege to speak. Rather than acknowledge the systemic violences that attempt to silence the rich voices, cultures, and histories that students bring into classrooms, this orientation positions students and,

by extension, the communities of students as eternally in need of institutional sanctioning.

2. **Paternalism was a huge part of the rationale for slavery.** When we operate with the mindset that we are "giving" students voice, we align ourselves with a deeply problematic and historical orientation. So much of the rationale for oppression through slavery, colonialism, and imperialism had to do with "giving" civilization to people who were "less fortunate." Do not align your pedagogy with the ethos of slavery and colonialism.

3. **They woke up like that.** When the young men at Rikers share their work, I am fully intimidated by their uses of extended metaphors, similes, and other literary devices. But all we did was lend them an ear. They woke up like that. We did not give them a voice. What we gave them was space to be heard. Students navigate powerful spaces of learning every single day in their homes and communities, especially when it comes to students of color, the skills, experiences, and rich knowledge that shape their voices are devalued in the classroom but are still powerful and have absolutely nothing to do with our "salvation."

Note

1. "If You Think You're Giving Students of Color a Voice, Get Over Yourself" by Jamila Lyiscott from *Medium* (blog), May 18, 2017, https://medium.com/@heinemann/if-you-think-youre-giving-students-of-color-a-voice-get-over-yourself-cc8a4a684f16. Copyright © 2017 by Jamila Lyiscott. Published by Heinemann, Portsmouth, NH. Reprinted by permission of the Publisher. All Rights Reserved.

4

Your Pedagogy Might Be More Aligned With Colonialism Than You Realize[1]

Berlin of 1884 was effected through the sword and the bullet. But the night of the sword and the bullet was followed by the morning of the chalk and the blackboard. . . . The bullet was the means of physical subjugation. Language was the means of spiritual subjugation.
—*Ngugi Wa Thiong'o*[2]

"I just had to stop you to say that you are *so* articulate!"

My 19-year-old self sat on a panel for a room full of high school seniors who eagerly sought insight about their transition to college, when a woman in the room cut me off mid-sentence to exclaim that I was *so* articulate. In the awkward silence that followed for a few seconds too long, my mind raced with confusion and a resounding discomfort . . . Thank you?

Of course, this remark was meant as a compliment, but what did her definition of *articulate* include? I imagined that if this woman heard me speaking with my father who sounds like he never left the islands of Trinidad and Tobago, would she have felt differently about my intellectual capacity? And if she heard me speaking Black English with my friends in Crown Heights, Brooklyn, would she have questioned my worth? And was being articulate while Black something exceptional (Alim and Smitherman, 2012)?[3] Yes, yes, and yes.

This woman was affirming my authority over Standard American English, and the truth is that I did, in fact, break out the finest formal English that my mind could conjure because I was in a school setting. The other languages that powerfully informed my linguistic identity—Black American English and Caribbean Creolized English—were silently prohibited from the space we shared. But why? And where did I learn to check my other languages at the door while in such settings?

What if I told you that prevailing attitudes toward the language practices that students bring into the classroom are rooted in colonial, often racist, logic? What if I told you that by not disrupting these kinds of attitudes in your classroom, your pedagogy might be more aligned with colonialism than you realize?

Well, I wrote the poem that would later become my first TED Talk, "3 Ways to Speak English," on the train ride home that same day. And this poem became the beginning of my journey toward exploring the intersections of language, race, and social justice as a critical social researcher, teacher educator, and community organizer.

The following is one of the most troubling findings to emerge from my research.

Ngugi Wa Thiong'o is an East African author who grew up in colonial Kenya and shares that a huge aspect of the colonial subjugation process was controlling the language of students in school, specifically that divorcing the language of the home/community from the space of school was a signature colonial tactic. In his book, *Decolonising the Mind*, he writes,

> One of the most humiliating experiences was to be caught speaking Gikuyu in the vicinity of the school. The culprit was given corporal punishment—three to five strokes of the cane on bare buttocks—or was made to carry a metal plate around the neck with inscriptions such as I

AM STUPID or I AM A DONKEY . . . what is important
. . . is that the language of our evening teach-ins, and
the language of our immediate community, and the language of our work in the field were one. . . . And then I
went to school, a colonial school, and this harmony was
broken. The language of my education was no longer the
language of my culture.

(Thiong'o, 1986, p. 111)[4]

When I came across this passage, I was shocked to learn that the
context of the colonial classroom was so similar to K–12 classrooms
across the United States today. No, students are not physically
beaten for speaking in the language of their communities, and
no, they are not forced to wear physical signs, but the work of
silencing, shaming, and severing the linguistic and cultural practices of the home in effort to have students adopt "Standard
American English" (SAE), purported to be the "language of
power," is the work of K–12 classrooms. And this colonial logic
is reinforced in our homes and communities under the false pre-
tense of arming children with access to a better world if only they
are willing to Ursula[5] their voices. A stance against white privilege
disrupts the malignant logic that Standard English is the language
of power, rendering other language practices powerless and void
of utility in K–12 classrooms. And a close look at young Ngugi's
testimony exposes how dangerously aligned our pedagogies are
with the subjugation tactics of colonization, which sought to police
the language of the oppressed peoples as a means of subjugating
their bodies. After all, Ngugi continues,

Berlin of 1884 was effected through the sword and the bullet. But the night of the sword and the bullet was followed
by the morning of the chalk and the blackboard. . . . The
bullet was the means of physical subjugation. Language
was the means of spiritual subjugation.

(Thiong'o, 1986, p. 9)[6]

The soldiers wielded the sword and the bullet. *Teachers* wielded the chalk and the blackboard. Arguments for how our educational institutions are governed by such marginalizing colonial practices rooted in white supremacy have been rigorously explicated. They are sound, and necessary, and valid, as well as lengthy, so we will reserve them for another day. But for today, there are still very powerful ways that linguistic diversity can be sustained to disrupt white privilege in your classroom.

Three Ways to Turn Your Classroom Into a Linguistic Celebration

Toward the end of "3 Ways to Speak English," I say, "Let there be no confusion, let there be no hesitation / This is not a promotion of ignorance, this is a linguistic celebration." This comes after what I hope is a clear social critique: that the three tongues that I engage in most frequently, "one for each: home, school, and friends," all inform my intellectual identity in uniquely powerful ways, and that any effort to diminish this is rooted in discrimination. This understanding guides my commitment to Culturally Sustaining Pedagogy (CSP) in my own practice as an educator. CSP is an approach that "seeks to perpetuate and foster—to sustain—linguistic, literate, and cultural pluralism as part of the democratic project of schooling (Paris, 2012, p. 93)."[7] Classrooms that seek to *sustain* linguistic, literate, and cultural pluralism are at once sites of "linguistic celebration." Here are three ways to begin shaping your classroom in this direction.

1. Check Your Attitude About the Multiple Language Practices of Your Students

As an educator, you probably have some pretty strong convictions about what constitutes excellence in your classroom. However, we do not often take the time to interrogate where our measures of excellence and standards are birthed. What makes the standard forms we uphold superior to other ways of knowing in our world? Standard Language Ideology is defined as "bias toward an abstracted, idealized, non-varying spoken language that is imposed and maintained by dominant institutions" (Lippi-Green, 2006).[8] What kinds of biased attitudes to you hold consciously and subconsciously about the languages your students engage in within their homes and communities? Are you complicit in upholding marginalizing social attitudes about language that are rooted in discrimination? Along with this, for the 21st-century student enmeshed in the digital landscapes and subsequent digital citizenship through media and technology, new digital literacies are in constant flux. If you have dismissed how the saturation of digital languages and literacies exist in the lives of your students, interrogate these attitudes.

2. Check Your Students' Attitudes About Their Multiple Language Practices

In an article titled "I Never Really Knew the History behind African American Language," Dr. April Baker-Bell shares her experiences engaging African American Language in the classroom:

> I recall having a discussion with my students about code-switching from AAL to Dominant American English (hereafter DAE). This discussion revealed that my students either held negative attitudes toward AAL (although they spoke it) or resisted using DAE because they felt that it reflected the dominant culture, and they did not want to be forced to imitate a culture of which they did not consider themselves part.
>
> (Baker-Bell, 2013, p. 355)[9]

Rather than make assumptions about your students' attitudes toward their own language practices, create critical, safe, and brave space to unpack what they already feel and know. If your racial, linguistic, or cultural identities differ from those of your students, be sure to regard this in how you plan and prepare for such space. Dominant ideologies have the capacity to seep into the consciousness to marginalized peoples, *and* marginalized people are not just passive objects of marginalization. So while it is news to some that the perspectives, languages, and cultural values of marginalized people are valuable, many of us know this and wrestle with what it means to navigate institutional spaces in light of these contradictions.

3. Put Voice Before Form

A mentor of mine once shared the philosophy of his first art teacher. On the first day of his art class, the teacher said to a classroom full of young minds, "I am not going to teach you how to paint, I am going to teach you how to see. Once you know how to see, you will be able to paint anything." We are so often fixated on the form that we want our students to master within the curriculum that we stifle the voices of our students. So many of my students have confided that they simply complete work to get the assignments of their teachers done. "What did you have to say about the question your teacher assigned?" I ask. "I don't know, I just said anything." Is your unit structured to put your students in dialogue with the disciplines of English, science, math, history, and so on? Or is it structured for your students to reproduce the form of a five-paragraph essay, for example, without time and space for learning what they actually have to say? What if students understood the classroom as a space where they were challenged to express voice and perspective in ways that draw on the various practices within their linguistic repertoires? What if SAE and five-paragraph essays were just two of many equally valuable forms in your classroom and your students, because you have *first* taught them how to *see* and how to critically and passionately tune into their own voice, are eager to master any form set before them?

Post-Chapter Optional Activity

Take a moment to listen to the TED Talk "3 Ways to Speak English." Imagine that a young Jamila and a young Ngugi are two new students in your classroom, transferring in from another time and space. Would your classroom be a space where the quality of being articulate is measured by monolithic standards? Would Ngugi flinch with shame and a deep sense of inferiority if his Gikuyu tongue slipped out? Or would your classroom be the linguistically and culturally affirming space we are so desperately in need of?

Notes

1. "Your Pedagogy Might Be More Aligned With Colonialism Than You Realize" by Jamila Lyiscott from *Medium* (blog), May 31, 2017, https://medium.com/@heinemann/your-pedagogy-might-be-more-aligned-with-colonialism-than-you-realize-1ae7ac6459ff. Copyright © 2017 by Jamila Lyiscott. Published by Heinemann, Portsmouth, NH. Reprinted by permission of the Publishers. All Rights Reserved.
2. Ngũgi, T. (1986). *Decolonising the Mind: The Politics of Language in African Literature.* London: J. Currey.
3. Alim, H. S., & Smitherman, G. (2012). *Articulate while Black: Barack Obama, language, and Race in the US.* Oxford: Oxford University Press, pp. xviii, 205.
4. See endnote 2.
5. In Hans Christian Andersen's *The Little Mermaid* the protagonist is offered access to a desirable world by the sea witch but only if she is willing to give up her voice in exchange.
6. See endnote 2.
7. Paris, D. (2012). Culturally sustaining pedagogy: A needed change instance, terminology, and practice. *Educational Researcher*, 41(3), 93–97.

8. Lippi-Green, R. (2006). Language ideology and language prejudice. In E. Finegan & J. R. Rickford (Eds.), *Language in the USA* (pp. 289–304). Cambridge: Cambridge University Press.
9. Baker-Bell, A. (2013). I never really knew the history behind African American Language: Critical language pedagogy in an advanced placement English language arts class. *Equity and Excellence in Education*, 46, 355–370.

5

Why Did All the Black Students Boycott My Classroom?

Why did all the Black students boycott my classroom?

Because I did not protect them
I was supposed to protect them
Because everywhere
Even here
We waited for their marrow
Their sinews
Their raw
Their pain
Was on the syllabus
For everyone to learn from
They were the diversity
We were the diversity
In every room concerned about justice
We became the curriculum
Unit by unit
A pedagogy made out of the oppressed

I did not protect them
When the racist comment was made from the back of the classroom
When it hurled itself at the young Black girl
When it hit her in the spirit and her eyes widened in horror
And I felt the widened silence of the room pivot toward me

I am Black
I am the professor
I am the Black professor

SURELY I am a racism slayer
An unapologetic racism warrior
Surely I have a sword sharp tongue
Surely I am prepared for this battle in a room
Where I am Black
I am the professor
I am the Black professor of Social Justice Education
Ha!
I am the Black professor who was hit in the spirit and my eyes
widened in horror too

Because everywhere else on campus they were stifled by racism
And this was supposed to be their oasis
A cool drink of water

Because in their small group work
Their Black vulnerability
Was always met with white silence
And "we couldn't take it anymore"
I listened in shame and silence

Too many moments of silence
Were supposed to be filled
With a swift defense against hatred

I am a bad professor
I am a bad protector

Did I shroud myself in silence
To coddle white comfort
Did I not unlearn this
I did not unlearn this
I was conditioned to keep white people comfortable
We were conditioned to keep white people comfortable
They don't even know that
We don't even know that

I am a bad professor
I am a bad protector
I am a bad professor of social justice education
I am a bad protector of social justice education
I couldn't even protect myself from the racist comment that was
hurled at us from the back of the classroom
Epic fail
I am sorry

Part II
Tools for Analysis and Action

For Freddie Gray

They broke our bones
And asked us not to break our silence
They stirred our embers
And when the fire erupted
They called it violence

6

T.H.U.G. L.I.F.E., Black Girl Magic, and Harry Potter

T.H.U.G. L.I.F.E.

Drawing on the sentiments of the 1960s' civil rights movement, on Friday, August 29, 2014, more than 600 Black people from throughout the country responded to a call for freedom rides to Ferguson, Missouri, after the murder of the unarmed teenager Michael Brown by officer Darren Wilson. A bus of about 40 of us from the New York City tristate area joined this call and took the 15-hour ride to share in the outrage, actions, and demands of local Ferguson activists on the ground.

As we marched down the streets of Ferguson, Missouri, nearing the spot where the lifeless body of 18-year-old Michael Brown had lain unattended for 4.5 hours . . . as we held our hands up in the universal sign of surrender while shouting, "HANDS UP! DON'T SHOOT!" . . . as I looked to my left and saw that marching alongside me were the tiny feet of a 4-year-old Black son holding onto a small "I Matter" sign and chanting with as much vigor as the Black elderly woman ahead of me who held onto her cane just as tightly . . . as we together proclaimed to the world with every fiber of our beings that if there is NO JUSTICE! there will be NO PEACE! . . . as we turned onto Canfield Drive and drew nearer to this spot where the blood of our son still stained the ground, the events that led up to this moment of protest attempted to clog my throat as they played over and over again in my mind.

On Saturday, August 9, an alarming tweet went out from rapper and Ferguson resident Thee Pharaoh.

As eyewitness to the murder, Pharaoh live-tweeted the tragedy over the next few hours for the entire Twitterverse.[1] His documentation served as a crucial component for the forthcoming explosion of protests and actions against racial injustice and police brutality across the nation.

He told us in frantic fear that he just saw someone die before his very eyes . . .

. . . The next tweet told us that he was moving into a state of hyperventilation . . .

. . . The next tweet revealed the horrifying unfolding reality . . . an officer just shot someone in front of his crib . . .

Primed by the highly publicized miscarriage of justice that unfolded following the murder of unarmed teenager Trayvon Martin and many other Black people over recent years, we tuned into the gruesome event as it unfolded and shared in the visceral impact that this real-time crisis was having on Pharaoh . . .

. . . He told us that the blood was all over the streets . . . that niggas was protestin' . . . police tape all over his building . . .

. . . He replied swiftly to the barrage of questions that followed on Twitter . . . why? . . . what did he do? . . . Nothing . . . he was running away! . . . The guy was running . . . the cops shot him in the back. . . . He saw him die bruh!

He was shaken . . . we were shaken . . .

We learned that Michael Brown was not posing any direct threat to the officers before his murder . . .

We learned that he was so, so young . . . that the victim's parents came out and started trippin' when they saw their murdered son . . .

And then, to add insult to injury, we learned that hours later, the body on the ground . . . A human. A son. A friend. A brother? A father? A student? . . . had received no medical attention or any attention at all from the surrounding authorities . . .

Over the next few days, a familiar trauma swept across Black America . . . one that has reminded us of the disposability of our bodies for more than 400 years. Darren Wilson murdered Michael Brown after Wilson ordered Brown and a friend to walk on the sidewalk and they refused. Eyewitnesses testified that Brown was moving away from Wilson, and after hearing the first shots ring out, he turned around and threw both hands up in surrender. In his testimony, Wilson insisted that he felt threatened by the unarmed teenager and shared that he felt no regret in his decision to shoot.

The protests and anger that erupted on the streets of Ferguson were unlike any concerted outburst against racial injustice in America that we had witnessed for decades. Led by young local residents of Ferguson, months and months of protests were intentionally sustained and met with a military presence that included tanks, machine guns, tear gas, and rubber bullets that were released onto protesters on the small residential streets of Ferguson. Very different accounts of these live events were fed to the public via mainstream media and social media. While mainstream media vilified Brown's character through images of him allegedly robbing a store and hypervisualized the small pool of protesters who were committing violent acts, Twitter, Facebook, and live-streamed videos from protesters on the ground told stories of excessive force by officers, of united outrage by the people who were taking a stand in their first amendment right, of a demand for answers, and of legitimate pain in the face of continuous racism against their community.

When we arrived in Ferguson from New York City 20 days after the murder, the military presence was gone, but the fight of the people and the newly armored police force were still very present. We heard first-person testimonies from Ferguson activists and spent three days together in collective action and vision for the Fergusons that exist all over our country.

On November 24, 2014, we watched and listened with pain that can hardly be described in words as the St. Louis County prosecutor announced that a grand jury decided not to indict Darren Wilson for this murder. We understood the moment in connection to a long history of racial hatred—disregard, abuse, inhumane treatment toward Black bodies and toward the substance of Black life—and so we hit the pavement in protest; we came together for comfort, healing, and demands that reflect the undeniable truth that Black Lives Matter.

The recurring articulation that "Black Lives Matter" throughout the 2014 social upheaval sparked by the death of Michael Brown in Ferguson, Missouri, is an indictment on the United States at large. The urgency of chanting, screaming, branding, and making viral this fundamental truth means simply that as a nation we have lived beneath the standard of this truth in policy, practice, procedure, and in everyday human interaction across disciplines. As we chant throughout the streets of Fergusons across the country and engage in the development and execution of both immediate and sustainable action in response to the lawful disposability and abuses against Black bodies, we do so to *inscribe* this powerful truth across ideological, discursive, institutional, and virtual landscapes. This inscription serves as a counter-hegemonic stance against the reality that white middle-class values and interests still serve as the substance of dominant culture, leaving little to no room for the values, ways of knowing, cultures, and practices of others, unless co-opted, of course. This inscription seeks to rewrite the dangerous single story (Adiche 2009)[2] that historically stigmatizes Blackness to death (literally) throughout the African Diaspora. And so, it exposes the need to center the already existing voices of Black people on Blackness and for new and safer stories that write Black lives into the narrative of humanity in rightful and righteous ways that are long overdue. It exposes the reality that "the future of the Black community is in our hands" (Sealey-Ruiz & Lewis, 2011e).[3]

When juxtaposed with the reality of a predominantly white and monolingual teaching force (Zumwalt & Craig, 2008)[4] and an increasing racially, culturally, and linguistically diverse student population (Aud et al., 2012; Paris & Alim, 2017),[5] we are forced to address the ways in which these social realities both produce and are produced by our systems of education. Critically centering the texts and sociocultural realities of marginalized groups in the classroom is one way to do this. Angela Thomas's *The Hate U Give* plays off Tupac's "The Hate U Give Little Infants F***s Everybody" (i.e., T.H.U.G. L.I.F.E.) to unpack how white privilege functions on both systemic and individual levels in the lives of youth of color and, ultimately, scars us all.

Black Girl Magic and Harry Potter

For racially marginalized youth who are inundated with ideologies that construct them as powerless, delinquent, and disposable, the impact of such viral stories is damaging in unimaginable ways. And because all things at some point in life become relevant to Harry Potter, I was inspired by Angie Thomas's allusions to Harry Potter in her sensational book *The Hate U Give* and took it upon myself to revisit J.K. Rowling's work for its relevance to the politics of race. To revisit the fact, that by nature of existing in his Muggle (i.e., non-magic humans) home, Harry was force-fed a narrative of being powerless, delinquent, and disposable. . . . To revisit, Harry's scar, a site of both pain and power, bore testimony of another world—a place of magic where his own power became central to his own narrative of healing and justice. Perhaps this is why Angie Thomas so beautifully invites us into a landscape where the Black female protagonist,

Starr, playfully calls herself Harry Potter as a child and then grows up to be a Black Girl Magical voice of resistance in the midst of Black disposability and police brutality.

Black Girl Magic is a philosophy and a movement started by CaShawn Thompson in 2013 in the face of dominant cultural messages that continue to cast Black women such as Serena Williams, Viola Davis, and Leslie Jones as aesthetically undesirable. Having its roots in, you guessed it, white supremacist thought, many Black women who do not fit into aesthetic or behavioral standards aligned with whiteness (i.e., light-skinned, slim, docile, passive, etc.) sit within the intersecting crossfire of both racial and gender oppression. Functioning together, these intersecting systems of oppression limit institutional access and possibilities for Black women globally. Black Girl Magic, as a movement, champions the fact that Black women have *still* managed to kill the game across disciplines, being named the most educated group in the United States by 2016! Angie Thomas and her protagonist, Starr, represent Black Girl Magic in beautifully disruptive and inspiring ways. So it is alongside the Black Girl Magic of Angie Thomas that I invite educators to disrupt white privilege in their classrooms; to imagine, for a second, that when viewed outside of the context of white supremacy, which constructs them as powerless, delinquent, and disposable, students of color and their communities carry their own magic, their own power and profound worth; and to imagine that maybe, Harry's scar (i.e., the symbol of Voldemort's impact on Harry's fate) can serve as a metaphor through which we can understand what happens when racially marginalized people are scarred by white privilege and we find ourselves wrestling with the spirit of Voldemort . . . I mean white privilege . . . that seeks to live inside of our consciousness and shackle the story of our magic.

In 1987, in their discussion of literacy development within and beyond schools, scholar-activists Freire and Macedo[6] asserted that reading and writing the word is preceded by reading and writing the world. The idea that it is possible to teach content in schools without careful attention to the contextual realities that students "read" in their worlds daily is absurd. *The Hate U Give* is an example of young adult literature that centers highly divisive sociopolitical issues in unapologetic ways. Many educators have dared to bring this polarizing conversation about police brutality into their classrooms through this text. This is a conversation that brings us toe-to-toe with white privilege given the alarming statistics that reveal the fates of white versus non-white people who come into contact with the police and given the alarming racial disparities that permeate our justice system to the point of it being named the New Jim Crow, or Slavery by Another Name. Within our increasingly politically polarized world, how do we engage ourselves and our students in critical conversations about what is happening around them? How do we equip them with the tools to read both the word and the world?

I want to offer Critical Literacy as a tool for engaging such work within and beyond our classroom. According to Ira Shor,[7] "Critical Literacy questions power relations, discourses, and identities in a world not yet finished, just, or humane. . . . Critical Literacy thus challenges the status quo in an effort to discover alternative paths for self and social development." Grounded in Critical Theory, Critical Literacy exposes how easily our society seeks to relegate us all to roles of passive consumers of our realities and invites oppressed groups to become agentive. Critical Literacy builds our capacity to decode and author the world around us.

Confronting White Privilege Through Critical Literacy: Freirian Culture Circles

In working with communities, educators, and scholars all over the country, I have utilized Paulo Freire's[8] culture circles as a means to engage other in the development of Critical Literacy skills to see and disrupt white privilege. Throughout the 1950s and 1960s, Freire worked closely with oppressed communities in Brazil through culture circles. As an arbiter of problem-posing education, Freire's approach to liberation through education challenges educators to reimagine classrooms as spaces where they function as co-creators of knowledge *with* students. This process necessitates wrestling with questions of inequity and oppression in ways that deepen the literacies and critical consciousness of all parties as they actualize themselves as subjects rather than objects of their realities. By its very nature, the Freirian culture circle demands both reflection and action as interwoven and has been used in powerful ways to reimagine pedagogical contexts all across the world.

The democratic practice of using this dialogue-to-action tool creates space for people across lines of difference to begin a deep reflection and dialogue about their immediate social reality. In order for the culture circle to be effective, teachers and other "authorities" in the space must challenge the traditional dynamics of power that govern classrooms in ways that seek to render students silent and empty. When working across lines of difference, it is crucial to first acknowledge and reflect on the varying social identities that will be in dialogue. In one experience facilitating a culture circle about police brutality, a white student became so enraged by the sight of the topic that she refused to engage in the conversation on the grounds that her father was a good police officer. In another experience, a man of color took up so much room speaking in the circle that you would have thought that the women in the space were mere extras in a movie where he was the star. And perhaps most frequently, with intergenerational culture circles where teachers and students are together, teachers often feel the need to fill the silence if students do not immediately speak and thereby reify the dynamic of teachers as the authoritative contributor in what is supposed to be a democratic context. To effectively participate in a culture circle, one must reflect deeply on the social identities that they carry and consider how these identities place him or her in sites of privilege and oppression in complex ways. And to effectively participate in a culture circle, one must challenge traditional markers of what counts as "knowledge" and understand that the experiential knowledge and non-Eurocentric ways of knowing that come from marginalized groups are valid sources for transformation, education, and liberation.

The process of the Freirian culture circle eventually brings groups to the point of designing collective action against the systemic and individual social ills that unfold through their analyses of their world. In the following, I describe each phase of the culture circle as it has unfolded in my own practice of using culture circles to confront white privilege.

Before you begin:

Culture circles begin with choosing a "code." A code is some kind of relevant cultural artifact that reflects the sociopolitics of the times. Newspaper clippings, art, memes, videos, quotes, and texts, among other items, may serve as a code. The code is chosen as the starting point of analysis. Critical Literacy is a lens, a pair of glasses that asks you to check and deepen the lens that you have been using to view the world around you. The code will be decoded throughout the process of dialogue in the culture circle and will eventually reveal the personal and institutional ramifications of social injustice before the final step of taking action. Using a large piece of chart paper, create six sections (one for each step) and have one person write notes within each section as the group engages in the guided dialogue.

Step 1: Description of Code

In the first step of the culture circle, a small group should look at the chosen code together. If a snapshot of *The Hate U Give* (either the book or the movie) were to serve as the code, all participants would enter into a discussion of what they notice without attaching any meaning. This step actually ends up being the most difficult for participants, in my experience. We are so smart that the act of observing without judging, of naming without blaming, of seeing without rushing to conclusions become quite the task. What this step powerfully reveals is the ways in which we allow our preconceived notions to constantly cloud our perception of the world around us. In a society inundated with white privilege, this means that all of us, white people *and* people of color, tend to perceive our world through the lens of whiteness, or the white gaze, because we have been conditioned to do so. Without doing the careful work of thinking about how deeply we have all internalized whiteness as rightness, we reinscribe white supremacy even in our efforts to disrupt it.

Step 2: First Analysis

This is the step where you can now attach meaning to what you described in step 1. Being mindful of the dynamics of the dialogue (i.e., Who is taking up a lot of space with their voice? Who is silent? Why?), collectively begin adding meaning to the items you've described. For one person, an American flag in the code might symbolize freedom. For another, an American flag might represent a history of oppression. Be sure to write it all down.

Step 3: Real Life

Within this step, you will now begin to make connections to your lived and/or witnessed reality. Here it is important to understand that when many social justice–oriented people come to the table, we do so with passionate analyses about systemic oppression and yadda, yadda, yadda. . . . What we are often blind to is the fact that each of us is positioned within the worlds of these realities. We are blind to our complicity. We are blind to our positionality. We are blind to the ways that these systems function in intersectional and ecological ways that show up in our daily realities. For white people, this step might reveal the ways that you unknowingly (or knowingly) benefit from white privilege in ways that undercut your public passion to fight against it. For people of color, this step might reveal the ways that you have internalized white supremacist thinking and uphold it within and beyond the classroom or the ways that your fears of addressing the impact of white privilege all around you have had detrimental effects on you and your students. So within this step, begin telling the stories of how the code connects to your personal life, what is happening in the news, in your community, your school, and so on.

Important note: Knowing what this step entails, be sure to determine *ahead of time* whether you wish to conduct this activity with interracial or monoracial groups. I have found both useful, depending on context. There are spaces in which folks need to go through this process within racial affinity groups and then share in a large-group discussion afterward.

Step 4: Related Problems

This step is crucial for understanding that no social issue stands alone. We live in an ecological world, an interdependent reality. Nature is interdependent, and so are we and the systems that we navigate. Related problems refer to the issues that surround the issue that is most obvious in the code. For example, a code about how white privilege is central to high dropout rates may not have any obvious evidence about mass incarceration, but you betta believe that these issues are deeply connected! Take some time as a group to reflect on issues that are related to what has already come up in the previous text.

Step 5: Root Causes

While step 4 asks you to look at the ecological, step 5 asks you to consider the historical/systemic/macro-rootedness of the issues that are unfolding in your discussion. Here, it is crucial to understand the power of an intersectional lens. Theorized by Kimberlé Crenshaw, intersectionality is a framework for understanding how intersecting systems of power work together against marginalized groups. This step in the Freirian culture circle reveals root causes such as "racism," "economic oppression," "classism," and, "sexism," for example. However, we live in a society where everyone who is racialized is also gendered, and everyone who is gendered exists within a specific economic reality. White privilege plays out differently depending on what systems of power are working together. For example, within *The Hate U Give* Starr moves between the socioeconomic realities of her community to the elite predominantly white context of her school daily. In this transition, Starr negotiates her racial identity in complex ways to survive in both contexts. To only focus on the root cause of racism and white privilege would limit our understanding of how economic oppression intersects with racism to shape the world of Starr and her community.

Step 6: Action

While this is the "final" step, the truth is that a Freirian approach to social justice requires continuous reflection *and* action. When Freire[9] conducted culture circles with over 300 sugarcane workers in Brazil to mobilize them around voting, literacy development, and other actions, the circles were so successful that they were halted by a military coup and Freire was jailed and exiled. Within this step, it is important to think collectively about what kind of action can be taken by the group to disrupt white privilege as it manifests itself in your immediate context. Naturally, the preceding steps will have taken you through a dialogue of very personal/individual insights, as well as the larger systemic realities that sustain and are sustained by white privilege. How will you confront white privilege through collective action?

Resource

Freire, Teaching, and Learning: Culture Circles Across Contexts (Counterpoints: Studies in the Postmodern Theory of Education) by Mariana Souto-Manning[10]

Notes

1. http://nymag.com/intelligencer/2014/08/man-may-have-live-tweeted-michael-brown-death.html
2. Adiche (2009). https://ted.com/talks/chimamanda_adichie_the_danger_of_a_single_story?language=en
3. Sealey-Ruiz, Y., & Lewis, C. (2011e). Passing the torch: The future of the Black community is in our hands. *Journal of Negro Education,* Epilogue, p. 426.
4. Zumwalt, K., & Craig, E. (2008). Who is teaching? Does it matter? In M. Cochran-Smith, S. Feiman-Nemser & J. McIntyre (Eds.), *Handbook of Research on Teacher Education: Enduring Questions in Changing Contexts* (3rd ed., pp. 404–423). New York: Routledge/Taylor & Francis Group.
5. Aud, S., Hussar, W., Johnson, F., Kena, G., Roth, E., Manning, E., . . Zhang, J. (2012). *The Condition of Education 2012 (NCES 2012-045).* Washington, DC: U.S. Department of Education, National Center for Education Statistics. Retrieved April 15, 2013, fromhttp://nces.ed.gov/pubsearch; Paris, D., & Alim, H. S. (2017). *Culturally Sustaining Pedagogies: Teaching and Learning for Justice in a Changing World.* New York, NY: Teachers College Press.
6. Freire, P., & Macedo, D. (1987). *Literacy: Reading the Word and the World.* West Port: Greenwood Publishing Group.
7. Shor, I. (2009). What is Critical Literacy. In *The Critical Pedagogy Reader* (pp. 282–304). New York: Routledge.
8. Souto-Manning, M. (2010). *Freire, Teaching, and Learning: Culture Circles Across Contexts.* New York: Peter Lang.
9. Freire, P. (1988). The Adult Literacy Process as Cultural Action for Freedom and Education and Conscientizacao. In Kintgen, E. R., Kroll, B. M., & Rose, M. (Eds.), *Perspectives on Literacy* (pp. 398–409). Carbondale, IL: Southern Illinois University Press.
10. See endnote 8.

7

The Politics of Ratchetness

The Politics of Ratchetness

Wretched
Just wretched
Ratchet
Madd ratchet
Madd ratchet yo
You. With your pants sagging
Low
Like our hope in an American dream
You. With your loud ratchet self
Neck twisting and turning like the Nile
Mouth smacking. Hands clapping.
With. Ev. ery. Word.
You with your skin so obscenely
And unapologetically Black
An onyx opulence
An ontological odyssey

Thick like the night
Black that blinds
Boogey man Black
You. With your skittles
And whatever is left of your spine
With your hands up
With your toy gun
You. With no arms
Because they are cuffed behind your back
And no arms
Because the threat of you lived only in their minds
You. With no breath
Because it has been stolen from your lungs
You. With your ghetto. violent. unruly. thuggish.
Ratchet self.
Wretched self.
Yo.

I love you.

8

Critical Hope in the Context of Crisis

It was 1845 when Frederick Douglass published his *own* narrative of freedom within the heinous climate of American chattel slavery. In a period where virtually all slave narratives were written and authenticated by white abolitionists to assure validity to a white readership, Douglass's title—*Narrative of the Life of Frederick Douglass, an American Slave, Written by Himself*—was a bold assertion. On one hand, literacy was forbidden for the enslaved, and the larger public imagination could barely fathom a Black person possessing the capacity to master formal English as articulately and as eloquently as Douglass had throughout all his writings. On the other hand, without an included statement of authentication from a white person in the opening pages, as was a standard feature of the slave narrative tradition, Douglass's story would be more readily disregarded as invalid by his white audience, who were already widely skeptical of the slave narratives that were penned and verified by white abolitionists. This commitment to penning his own story was an unapologetic extension of his physical, mental, and linguistic fugitivity from the systemic oppressions of slavery. This assertion of authorship and authority over his own voice within a historical moment where his very flesh was supposed to be owned by others was a crucial disruption for America's national consciousness, which still rings with deep relevance in today's society where the mainstream ideologies about communities of color that perpetuate social inequities are hardly, if ever, authored by members of those communities. For Douglass, voice, authorship, and his own fugitive literacies became the means by which he attained multiple freedoms throughout his lifetime. A lifetime dedicated to critically explicating the personal and broader systemic violences of slavery through his writings and speeches across the nation. His narrative's description of the indelible impact of slavery conditions on his feet is arguably one of the most compelling examples of this. He writes,

> I was seldom whipped by my old master, and suffered little from anything else than hunger and cold. I suffered much from hunger, but much more from cold. . . . My feet have been so cracked with the frost, that the pen with which I am writing might be laid in the gashes.
>
> (Douglass, 1846, p. 72)

As Douglass articulates the *context* of slavery—harsh winters where the enslaved were forced to sleep outside with barely any clothes on—he conjures up the visceral imagery of brokenness in his cracked feet to paint a picture of how this context played out on his individual person. His next rhetorical move—that of bringing together his pen with his gashes—illustrates how the intimacy of language, voice, and authorship are enmeshed with his story of bondage and freedom. This iterative relationship between pen and feet has resounding symbolic value that at once textualizes the body and animates the text. What this imagery then affords us is the assertion that the social context of slavery in Douglass's time, embodied by his feet, was inextricably bound to his literate identity, symbolized by his pen. By placing the pen into the brokenness of his feet, a powerful possibility of wholeness is evoked even as the impact of systemic oppression still exists on his broken body. My Fugitive Action Framework builds on this powerful imagery with the conviction that within the crises of our times there is critical hope in the power of authorship.

Fugitivity

"Wait a minute, when we go to high schools to recruit students, we only recruit Black students to be athletes here . . ." The room fell into a thick silence, and a palpable tension crept across the small lecture hall on a tiny college campus in upstate New York. After spending some time with the Fugitive Action Framework, the all-white faculty and staff in the room were confronted with the reality that their institution had some glaring racial disparities that they could no longer ignore. The troubling conversation that just unfolded was around the realization that all their Black and Brown students sit together in the cafeteria (shout out to Beverly Tatum's work!) and do not participate in much else on campus. "You mean you're not going into high schools to recruit Black students to do astrophysics here?" My satirical comment was met with a few scattered awkward chuckles. I continued: "What ideologies, what silent practices and norms are at play here if the already small number of Black and Brown students you have in this Predominantly White Institution are moving in huddled silos?" A small nervous voice chimed in from the back of the room, "I have asked a few of them . . . they said that they don't feel comfortable here."

Because the United States is pretty much as segregated now as it has ever been, glaring statistics that reflect this segregation mark P–16 institutions across the nation, myriad educational inequities emerge out of the racial and economic disparities that cause P–12 schools in lower and working-class communities of color to be severely under-resourced and structurally stagnated. In response to this, countless efforts to get Black and Brown students of color into college have been celebrated as the hallmarks of success. In our obsession with "college and career readiness," getting Black and Brown students accepted into Predominantly White Institutions (even after being raised within deeply seg-regated communities and school district) becomes the ultimate goal. And when they get there, they suffer in ways that we have yet to truly address.

We go sooo hard to get Black and Brown youth out of the physical violence of the streets without equipping them for the psychological and emotional violences they will have to navigate to survive within institutions that were originally built without them in mind. In order to survive predominantly white schools, people of color know intuitively that "access" means assimila-tion and that "excellence" means erasure of the self. Yet, our systems of education are often force-fed to us as politically and ideologically neutral spaces that seek to propel anyone forward if only they would "pull themselves up by their bootstraps." These lies are nothing short of gaslighting for students such as the ones mentioned earlier, who navigate predominantly white contexts with a deep sense of fugitivity.

During American chattel slavery, the vision for freedom was first borne in the mind of the fugitive. In pursuit of that freedom, fugitives had to imagine themselves outside of the narrative that slavery sought to impose on their humanity. Fugitivity was a narrative of its own, one which acknowledged a broken past but was driven by an unrelenting hope for a whole future. Fugitivity disrupted white authority over Black bodies and authored pos-sibilities beyond the permission of white power. Drawing on my research and practice around questions of white privilege, mul-tiple literacies, and racial justice, the Fugitive Action Framework works to confront and transform the authority and authorship of white privilege as it exists on both macro (systemic) and micro (individual) levels within our society. Through principles of analysis and action, this framework seeks to actualize the agency and healing of the pen as it is laid in the gashes of a history fraught with racial and intersecting oppressions. In the context of our present-day political crises that unabashedly promote white privilege, xenophobia, and hate, the Fugitive Action Framework works in the service of what Jeffrey Duncan-Andrade calls "Critical Hope."[1] I recently read a tweet that said "[H]ope is a narcotic for the oppressed." Empty, flowery abstract notions of hope do nothing for the immediate oppressions weighing on people of color in this country. Critical hope is tangible and active hope. Duncan-Andrade writes,

> On the flipside of these false hopes lies critical hope, which rejects the despair of hopelessness and the false hopes of "cheap American optimism" (West, 2008, p. 41). Critical hope demands a committed and active struggle "against the evidence in order to change the deadly tides of wealth inequality, group xenophobia, and personal despair".
> (West, 2004, pp. 296–297, quoted in Duncan-Andrade, 2009)

Fugitive Action Framework

My Fugitive Action Framework was adapted from the "Four 'I's' of Oppression" as developed by several grassroots youth organizations.[2] I came to develop this framework as a tool for working closely through critical analysis, activism, and advocacy work with educators, students, and community members across the nation to acknowledges that oppression in our society functions on both systemic and individual levels as indicated in Figure 8.1. That is, in order to understand the flow and impact of white privilege, one cannot only view the most visible manifestations of social ills as they occur to the naked eye as problematic. Everyday micro-level manifestations of white privilege are symptomatic of much-deeper macro-level issues in our world. It is important to

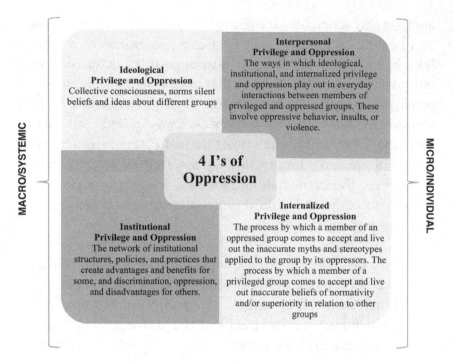

Ideological Privilege and Oppression
Collective consciousness, norms silent beliefs and ideas about different groups

Interpersonal Privilege and Oppression
The ways in which ideological, institutional, and internalized privilege and oppression play out in everyday interactions between members of privileged and oppressed groups. These involve oppressive behavior, insults, or violence.

4 I's of Oppression

Institutional Privilege and Oppression
The network of institutional structures, policies, and practices that create advantages and benefits for some, and discrimination, oppression, and disadvantages for others.

Internalized Privilege and Oppression
The process by which a member of an oppressed group comes to accept and live out the inaccurate myths and stereotypes applied to the group by its oppressors. The process by which a member of a privileged group comes to accept and live out inaccurate beliefs of normativity and/or superiority in relation to other groups

MACRO/SYSTEMIC

MICRO/INDIVIDUAL

FIGURE 8.1 Adapted from Global Action Project's 4 I's of Oppression

understand that these levels are interdependent. For example, racist jokes about students in the teachers' lounge occur at the micro level, while disproportionate suspension rates for students of color function at the macro level. Taken together, these two seemingly disconnected issues deeply inform each other. The problem is that even when we do perceive the manifestation of white privilege on the micro level in our everyday realities, we do not account for how situations fit into the larger systemic-level violences that undergird the very fabric of our society.

The Fugitive Action Framework provides a lens for critically analyzing the presence of white privilege and oppression in any social situation. When I became a spoken word artist at the age of 15, I quickly learned that my success in the genre required me to cultivate a poetic lens. I consumed a wide range of poetry and began to consider the metaphorical value of all phenomena—the way that a plane is borne and must break through the opacity of clouds before it can hit clear skies (perhaps our moments of deepest confusion are necessary before we can have a breakthrough), the way that the branches of trees mirror its roots (perhaps how we branch out into the world is a metaphysical reflection of where we came from), the way that an old cell phone does not have the capacity to download new software updates and old software does not work on new cell phones (perhaps we need to update our archaic educational system so that it has the capacity to sustain an upgrade of equity and justice for all). All around me was poetry. Carefully cultivating this lens reshaped the way that I see the world around me like a pair of glasses, without which I would be blind. This framework is not a solution to white privilege and its ugly cousin, racism. It is not a tool for binding and gagging white privilege, locking it up, and throwing away the key before dusting off our hands and moving on to something else. Instead, this framework invites the cultivation of new forms of racial literacy, that is, developing new skills for "reading" white privilege as it exists in the world and for "writing/authoring" a future that combats white privilege by sustaining cultural pluralism in systemic and individual ways.

The 4 "I's" of Oppression as they have been previously theorized are Ideological, Institutional, Interpersonal, and Internal. The Ideological and Institutional levels speak to the systemic/macro nature of the flow of oppression while the Interpersonal and Internal levels speak to the individual/micro nature of oppression:

IDEOLOGICAL Privilege and Oppression: Collective consciousness, norms silent beliefs and ideas about different groups.

INSTITUTIONAL Privilege and Oppression: The network of institutional structures, policies, and practices that create advantages and benefits for some, and discrimination, oppression, and disadvantages for others (institutions are organized bodies such as companies, governmental bodies, prisons, schools, non-governmental organizations, families, and religious institutions, among others).

INTERPERSONAL Privilege and Oppression: The ways in which ideological, institutional, and internalized privilege and oppression play out in everyday interactions between members of privileged and oppressed groups. These involve oppressive behavior, insults, or violence.

INTERNALIZED Privilege and Oppression: The process by which a member of an oppressed group comes to accept and live out the inaccurate myths and stereotypes applied to the group by its oppressors; the process by which a member of a privileged group comes to accept and live out inaccurate beliefs of normativity and/or superiority in relation to other groups.

Figure 8.2 offers an example of how the 4 I's of oppression might explain some common in-school practices.

In order to effectively utilize the Fugitive Action Framework to analyze and act against white privilege within and beyond the classroom, we can view the 4 I's as tools for analysis and action by following these steps (Figure 8.3):

Before you begin.

Decide on a racially charged situation that occurred at your institution, in your home, on the news, on social media, and so on. This situation will be the starting point of your analysis.

Learning to "read" white privilege.

The analysis stage of the framework will involve you learning how to read white privilege as it manifests itself across the 4 I's of the framework. Employing the framework with others is ideal, but be sure to determine *ahead of time* whether you would like to do this work in interracial or monoracial contexts.

MACRO/SYSTEMIC

**Ideological
Privilege and Oppression**
Students of color are only intellectually valuable contributors to society when they align themselves with Eurocentric/white middle class norms

**Interpersonal
Privilege and Oppression**
Oppression: The student engages in acts of cultural/linguistic erasure; the student is silent or oppositional; the student passively accepts

Privilege: The teacher "gives" students voice

4 I's of
Oppression
(Examples)

**Institutional
Privilege and Oppression**
Pedagogies, policies, and practices that perpetuate savior-complex, ignore knowledges of marginalized communities, and frame students as deficient/delinquent when they are "not competent" by Eurocentric standards

**Internalized
Privilege and Oppression**
Oppression: "My voice comes from outside of myself and my community; Voice must be given to me by an institution or an authority figure to be valid"
Privilege: "Students of color need to be given tools for a voice that sounds like appropriate Eurocentric practices so that we can hear them; I have successfully saved these students of color"

MICRO/INDIVIDUAL

FIGURE 8.2 Example of how the 4 I's might play out

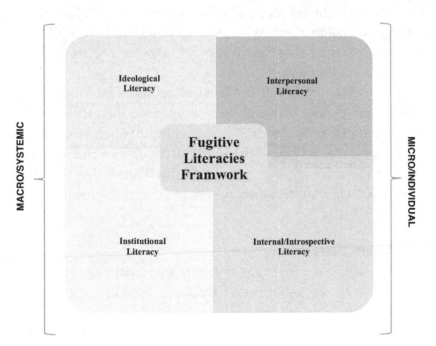

MACRO/SYSTEMIC

Ideological
Literacy

Interpersonal
Literacy

Fugitive
Literacies
Framwork

Institutional
Literacy

Internal/Introspective
Literacy

MICRO/INDIVIDUAL

FIGURE 8.3 Fugitive Action Framework

Ideological Literacy

With your group, analyze the chosen situation for any silent collective norms that center white privilege. For example, this past graduation season, a viral image from a South Carolina high school read "Since graduation is a dignified and solemn occasion, graduating seniors and their guests should behave appropriately." The sign went on to say that anyone who did not comply would be charged a fine of up to $1,030. Let me save you some time, this sign is racist! To conceive of graduation as a "dignified and solemn occasion" is deeply Eurocentric and marginalizing for the countless cultural practices that view celebrations and milestones as opportunities to turn allll the way up. Where I'm from, being dignified and solemn during a time of celebration would be a cause to call security on *you*! Within this sign, are silent collective norms that are "appropriate" according to white middle-class values. Identifying white privilege as it functions on the ideological level is crucial! It is this level that is most abiding and informed by the dark histories of slavery and colonialism. What we accept as "normal" and "neutral" immediately casts the ways of knowing and of being people of color as delinquent.

Ideological literacy at the level of action is a bit tricky. Ideologies are far more abstract and ubiquitous than the other I's. But by naming the problematic ideologies that perpetuate white supremacy, we can *author* the kinds of ideologies that we envision for racial equity and justice with the knowledge that these ideologies will manifest themselves in powerfully healing ways across the 4 I's.

Institutional Literacy

At this level, it is important to know that institutional policies and practices are undergirded by the very white supremacist ideologies that we all buy into as normal. For example, two young Black girls were suspended from their Massachusetts high school for wearing braids in their hair. Let me save you some time . . . this is racist! Just as the institution in the previous example acted in the service of ideologies that are saturated with white privilege, these girls were punished for breaking their school's *policy* of what is "appropriate" for hair and dress code. Braided extensions are basically the epitome of Black-girlness. At an institutional level, the ideologies of white aesthetics as appropriate are enforced through institutional policy. Again, developing an "institutional literacy" is a way to "read" the ways that white privilege plays out on an institutional level. It is at this level of literacy that the faculty members in the preceding example were able to "read" that their institution recruits Black students only for their sports teams and then are confused about why all their degree programs lack racial diversity.

Institutional literacy at the level of action means disrupting the institutional policies that propel white supremacy. It means taking the active steps necessary to restructure, rewrite, and reimagine your institution as a racial and culturally inclusive space that does not stop at having bodies of color in the room as long as they behave "appropriately." Rather, institutional literacy at the level of action means that it is time to envision and author our institutions as spaces where white privilege cannot survive.

Interpersonal Literacy

Interpersonal literacy, at the level of analysis, is any opportunity to "read" the relationships in any given situation. For example, when a large white male police officer presses his knee into the back of a 12-year-old Black girl in a bathing suit for being at a pool party in a white neighborhood, there is an interpersonal dynamic that occurs between the officer and the young girl. This interpersonal dynamic is only made possible by a justice system (institution) that blatantly upholds policies and practices that assure us that Black and Brown bodies are disposable (ideology) in this country. Similar interpersonal dynamics marked by white privilege play out in schools between teachers and students. Currently, more than 83% of urban educators are white, yet the racial disparities between teachers and students that bear on classroom spaces are hardly, if ever, addressed. At this level of analysis, analyze your chosen situation for the interpersonal dynamics at play and try to see how they are legitimated by institutional norms and how those institutional norms are rooted in toxic white privilege ideologies.

Interpersonal literacy, at the level of action, means addressing the interpersonal dynamics that occur in your world in deeply problematic ways. Perhaps you are a person of color who finds yourself enforcing rigid behavioral standards on students of color that are aligned with institutional policies that you are forced to uphold. Perhaps you are a white authority figure who responds differently to the emotional outbursts of white youth vs youth of color. Perhaps you are a parent who is tired of your Black or Brown baby coming home with the feeling that he or she is being over punished and over-labeled for simply being youthful. At this level, the action is meant to reimagine and take action in the areas of the interpersonal dynamics that support white privilege.

Internal/Introspective Literacy

Internal/introspective literacy, at the level of analysis, means doing the deep self-awareness work to learn how white privilege roots itself in our very consciousness. I say "our" because people of color who internalize white privilege as normal, can and do function in ways that sustain white privilege. For me, this is the most dangerous level. What did the 12-year-old girl with an officer's knee pressing into her back internalize about her worth on that day? And for the millions of people who viewed the viral video, what did we internalize about the value of Black bodies in this country? Doing the introspective work to "read" your internal state is key. It is impossible to do the work of acting against white privilege in the world if you are not concurrently doing the work of acting against white privilege in yourself.

At the level of action, internal/introspective literacy is about changing yourself in an anti-racist, pro-cultural pluralism agent of racial justice. It means that you take action against the ideologies, institutional practices, and interpersonal reinforcements that have embedded themselves into your consciousness so that you now function in the service of white privilege (whether you are white or not).

Notes

1. Duncan-Andrade, J. (2009). Note to educators: Hope required when growing roses in concrete. *Harvard Educational Review* 79(2), 181–194.
2. The Fugitive Action framework is adapted from Global Action Project's version of this.

9

Why I Started Using Cyphers for Justice

Every semester that I teach educators on topics ranging from diversity to racial justice to achievement in urban schools, I make sure to include a unit on the art of the cypher.

For those who don't know, over 83% of our urban educators are not people of color and live outside of the racially diverse communities where their students reside.

So I bring in the cypher, a practice within hip-hop culture with West African roots.

Essentially, it's a circle of people who come together to share in extemporaneous freestyle or newly written ideas over a beat.

The goal is to exhibit mastery
Lyrical and rhetorical dexterity
Sometimes using the African Diasporic tradition of signifying

*So every semester for some years now I have taught these teach-
ers some fundamental skills and features of hip-hop writing so that
they dare participate in the art of the cypher*

*And every semester I witness the same exact patterns during the
lesson . . .*
In a nutshell, panic and fear

*The beat is in the background and as I watch the anxiety and hesitation
in the room reach a boiling point I lower the music to invite some truth
Honest reflection about what is being felt*

*Vulnerability, fear of failure, discomfort about being inauthentic,
my lines suck!*
These are some of the feelings that are agreed upon in the room

It is at this point
When I can see the anxious excitement of some
And fear and shame in the eyes of others that I ask

*How many of your students do you label illiterate by societal standards
While they can demonstrate mastery over this complex form that
intimidates YOU in this cypher?*

*How inauthentic it must feel for them to speak in a language that
regards their own as inferior?*

*I tell this 83% that for marginalized peoples, a truly diverse society
is not about simply being included in dominant culture*

I tell them that
I am a repository of a transnational conflict

Have you ever endured the duplicity of feeling like both victim and convict?
Have you ever endured the shame of mixing your words with your thoughts?
Like 'professor, this author purports that sometimes hegemonic forces are forced to use degrees of fabrication
And I be thinkin' the same thing so I don't know why they be hatin"
This may sound like another case of broken English
But I be as broken as the records of our histories so I'll be that broken record
I be that broken record
Can you see my lines?

There be freedom in my broken
There be wholeness in my lines
There be wholeness in my broken
There is freedom in these lines

I tell them that the process toward diversity is not just about the presence of difference
It is about creating spaces and opportunities for truly esteeming and exploring the value of difference on its own terms

You see the problem with standard forms is not that we are incapable of acquiring them
It is that they so often fail to incorporate the genius that is available within diverse cultures
And when I am forced to be like you then I am robbed
And you are robbed
Of the fullest potential of me

"Whew chile!"= A Black (American Black) expression of surprise, exasperation, or an appropriate response after just gettin' the tea.[1] My session in a Midwest professional development series with in-school and out-of-school educators wanting to make the initiatives of Black Lives Matter relevant to their classrooms was definitely a "whew chile" moment.

"But where do I find the hip-hop that is safe to show the youth that I work with? I like the music, but it's hard to find the kind of hip-hop that does not glorify prison culture." The veteran white teacher in the group shared her deep concern for trying to access hip-hop culture in ways that feel "decent."

"I see a few nods around the room," I respond. "But I want to push back on some of the deeper conditioning that informs your question. This is why we are here, right? To confront our conditioning in real ways, yeah?" More nods.

"So let me ask you this: How safe or possible is it for us to teach our children about Thomas Jefferson and Christopher Columbus without glorifying slavery and genocide?"

Whew chile!

Most people in the United States are more decisively offended by a pair of sagging pants than police brutality. Most people in the United States are more alarmed by their perception of prison culture (i.e., baggy/sagging clothes, profanity, gang signs, etc.) than by the system violences of the prison industrial complex. In the same vein, our preconceived notions about what violence and vulgarity look like in our society make it difficult for many educators to truly value hip-hop culture. Despite a long history of research and practice pointing to the profound value of using culturally relevant content in the classroom, our perceptions remain steeped in historical conditioning and commitments to whiteness—the norms, standards, and values that govern schooling—so that we view sagging pants as a threat when the people in our world who are truly at the helm of global violence wear a suit and tie every single day. And for those of us who are actively committed to disrupting in-school norms, the weight of expectations around standards and testing stifle us into the cookie cutter struggle of teaching curriculum that is painful to uphold. These are some of the reasons why I started using cyphers with educators and students across the country.

My commitment to the profound pedagogical value of cyphers is inspired by my work with the Cyphers for Justice program in New York City. Cyphers for Justice is a youth-led program where a team of youth and adult allies[2] collaborate on research and activism through the lens of hip-hop, spoken word, and critical media literacy. Within hip-hop, the cypher is a cultural practice borne out of resistance, resilience, and the sheer brilliance (Bars!) of Black and Brown youth. While its history is rooted in West African traditions, the early 1980s served as the stage on which rap battles in the form of cyphers took off across marginal spaces where voices usually went unheard. Intentionally, the word *cipher*, sometimes spelled *cypher*, derives from the word decipher so that in order for you to effectively decode or decipher what a given rapper is saying, you must be "hip" (i.e., *hip* = knowledgeable about the times; *hop* = constant movement) to the esoteric knowledge within the culture. This means that in order for your bars to be hot, they must contain ingredients, such as powerful literary devices, shade, and enigmatic cleverness. One popular example is the "real gs" line from Lil Wayne's song "6 Foot 7 Foot"; for the lyrics, see https://genius.com/Lil-wayne-6-foot-7-foot-lyrics. Hip-hop in its rawest form is antihegemonic. Hip-hop in its rawest form disrupts white privilege. So I bring it with me everywhere I go.

The caricature of "yo, yo, yo . . . b****, h***, n*****" often centered in the mainstream flattens the beautiful nuanced complexities of hip-hop culture. Any inclination to reduce hip-hop to this description falls in rhythm with every historical attempt to stigmatize the cultural contributions of people of color who do not readily fit the palate of whiteness. Does this mean that we ignore the myriad violences that exist within hip-hop culture? No. We understand them as an unapologetic mirror held up to our society. A Culturally Sustaining Pedagogical approach to engaging hip-hop culture will have us know that in our quest to be more equitable, it is dangerous to fetishize or flatten the marginal cultural practices that we seek to bring into our classrooms. So you better believe that the moment my students and I begin unpacking the sexism and toxic masculinity in hip-hop, we simultaneously analyze the sexism and toxic masculinity in Shakespeare!

You see, in part, my goal in working with educators around challenging traditional teaching and learning practices is to have us take a look at each of our unit goals and articulate our *own* personal pedagogical goals and standards for each lesson plan. So, if you are an educator who is committed to equity, the common core standard of determining the theme and central idea of a text, for example, MUST fit within *your own standard* of sustaining opportunities for students to engage with diverse texts. Citing evidence and determining the central idea of a text within hip-hop requires the same (and sometimes even more complex) cognitive skills as a traditional text.

I use cyphers to expose the visceral discomfort of engaging with cultural practices that feel foreign to the archaic terrain of traditional schooling. It forces many teachers into the vulnerability of feeling like learners of something new and invites other teachers who already engage with hip-hop culture to challenge the taboo of creating room for it in their classrooms.

I use cyphers to style on whiteness by celebrating the creative, intellectually rigorous, and transformative possibilities that exist in hip-hop, but remain largely ignored because of our rigid convictions about what is appropriate and valuable for teaching and learning. During one session a teacher asked, "What if I don't have mastery over genres like hip-hop and spoken word?" "Were you born with mastery over the five paragraph essay?" I quipped. The answer was, of course, no. Yet without question, we become students of the skills, genres, and norms that we value as a society.

I use cyphers to model that hip-hop culture has its own inherent rigor and value and should not be engaged as a bait and switch for hooking students into the "real content."

I use cyphers as a pre-unit activity to access the background knowledge of students. When they spit bars, they spit gems of knowledge that support me in understanding their schema or the ways they already understand some of the content that I hope to explore with them. And accessing this knowledge helps me to revise my units in light of what I have learned from them.

If you want to draw on hip-hop culture to reimagine what teaching and learning might look like in your classroom and/or to trouble your own internalized oppression or privilege, which limits how you might view hip-hop culture, interrogate your own racial/ethnic/linguistic/economic identities and how they inform your perceptions and relationship to hip-hop. What does this reveal about your comfort and capacity to engage hip-hop culture in your classroom? Then, set out to become a student of hip-hop culture. Immerse yourself in the history, theories, and practical classroom resources that you may have previously disregarded. While I trouble up some issues here to reveal the utility of using cyphers and hip-hop for justice in my work, a truly meaningful understanding of how you might take up hip-hop in your pedagogy will only come out of a deep study of the culture, scholars, and practitioners of hip-hop pedagogy.

Notes

1. Not hot water and leaves.
2. Adults within Cyphers for Justice are referred to as "adult allies" in alignment with the youth-led philosophy of Youth Participatory Action Research, which deeply informs the program.

Afterword

I grew up on the intersection of Jefferson Avenue and Marcus Garvey Avenue in Brooklyn, New York. At the intersection of slave owner and liberation leader. At the intersection of white supremacy and Black power. Healing is not the absence of wounds. This is why in the work of *Black Appetite. White Food.* it is important to acknowledge the complex coexistence of pain and possibility. For me, the work of navigating the pain and possibility of racial justice, equity, hope and fighting for humanization in an often-dehumanizing world have become deeply personal. I have found that forging forward in my quest toward justice has been inextricably bound to my own quest toward understanding the intergenerational trauma in my family. It turns out that my journey toward educational justice has turned powerfully inward, a lens into my own complicated humanity.

I did not find out that my mother was a survivor of sexual abuse until I was 31 years old. Apparently, she had blocked the trauma out of her memory; her will to bury her past was matched only by her passion for creating a future of possibilities for me, her only child. Here I was traveling the world, a scholar-activist bent on promoting equity and justice as much as possible, vehemently opposed to every iteration of racial injustice as it intersects with other systems of oppression, but in my home . . . in my own legacy . . . in my own mother lay a pain that I did not have words for. Suddenly *social* justice did not feel as urgent. I wanted personal justice. Suddenly my racial and gender identities felt a million times heavier than ever before. Suddenly I could not take in another social media or mainstream media story of Me Too . . . *you* too, Mommy?! I learned that there was an entire legacy of sexual assault endured by the matriarchs of my family and soon found myself hard-pressed to find anyone who was not either a survivor or related to one. Navigating the work of social justice in the classroom and in the community is bound up with our own personal histories that cannot be divorced from how we show up in the work and in the world.

Black Appetite. White Food. Represents the tension of healing and questing toward (educational) justice in a world that struggles deeply to see beyond the scope of white supremacy. It is a lens into the power that our cultures and communities have long possessed, the audacity of our survival, and our insistence on thriving in spite of the abiding oppressions that pervade systems of education. This is what I invite—not sweeping victories or the neat dismantling of racial injustices but the messiness of the inner and outer work that nourishes our appetites peace, equity, and palpable justice.

CPSIA information can be obtained
at www.ICGtesting.com
Printed in the USA
BVHW041803281121
622723BV00027B/892

9 781138 480667